I0459109

MAVERICK RISING

Rebelling with purpose to fulfill your divine destiny

ADEBAYO NATHANIEL ADEMOLA

MAVERICK RISING

Copyright ©2025 by Adebayo Nathaniel Ademola

Paperback ISBN: 978-1-965593-69-1

All rights reserved. No part of this publication may be reproduced, distributed, or transmitted in any form or by any means, including photocopying, recording, or other electronic or mechanical methods without the prior written permission of the author except in the case of brief quotations embodied in reviews and certain other non-commercial uses permitted by copyright law.

Published by Cornerstone Publishing

A Division of Cornerstone Creativity Group LLC
Info@thecornerstonepublishers.com
www.thecornerstonepublishers.com

Author's Contact

To book the author to speak at your next event or to order bulk copies of this book, please, use the information below:

Email: adebayonathaniel208@gmail.com

Printed in the United States of America.

DEDICATION

To every maverick at heart, those who refuse to be defined by limits, who dare to rise when others settle, and who choose obedience to God over the comfort of the crowd.

This is for you.

May your courage to stand apart ignite others to discover and walk in their divine destiny.

To the One who called me out of conformity into purpose, To Jesus Christ, my Master and Model of true rebellion, obedient unto death, yet triumphant in destiny.

CONTENTS

ACKNOWLEDGMENTS

This book is a testament to grace, the unrelenting grace of God that transforms ordinary lives into divine instruments of purpose.

I deeply appreciate the leading of the Holy Spirit, whose wisdom, conviction, and inspiration birthed every word of Maverick Rising.

My heartfelt gratitude goes to my loving wife, Mrs. Mercy Adebayo, and our wonderful children, Jonathan, Joana and Joyce Adebayo, for your love, patience, and unwavering support. You are my daily reminder that purpose is best lived out through love and family.

To my lovely mum, Mrs. Sarah Abel, thank you for your prayers, sacrifices, and endless encouragement. You have been a pillar of faith and strength.

To my amazing siblings, Blessing, Victoria, and Marvellous, thank you for standing by me and cheering me on through every season.

To my mentors and spiritual guides who shaped my understanding of purpose and destiny, and to every friend and supporter who encouraged me along this journey, your faith in me has been invaluable.

Finally, to every reader who dares to rise, may this book remind you that you were not created to blend in. You were born to stand out and fulfill your divine destiny.

INTRODUCTION

From time to time, everyone gets to the point of wondering whether there is more to life than what they see and experience daily. You may not always put it into words, but deep inside, you may feel the sense that you were not created just to survive, follow routines, or blend into the background of everyone else's story. You feel a stirring within for something deeper, something braver, something that dares to break the mould. That stirring is what we call the maverick spirit.

Sadly, most people do not yield to this inward stirring. They let fear, doubt, and the pressure to "fit in" dictate the rhythm of their lives. They hide their questions, bury their dreams, and convince themselves that playing it safe is the wiser choice. Yet, history proves otherwise. Progress never comes from those who blend into the crowd; it comes from those who dare to step out.

Activating the maverick spirit doesn't mean you have to be louder, stronger, or more talented than everyone else. It simply means you're willing to see life differently and to live with the courage to follow that vision, even when it costs you something. It's not about perfection; it's about action fuelled by conviction.

Maybe you've felt too ordinary to carry that kind of spirit. Maybe you've doubted yourself or convinced yourself that mavericks are "other people" - the bold, the brilliant, the born leaders. But here's the surprise: the maverick spirit isn't reserved for a chosen few. It's already within you, waiting to be activated. The question is, will you let it out?

This book is an invitation to do just that. To let the fire inside you rise. To challenge the normal patterns that hold you back. To discover that you don't have to wait for ideal circumstances, or for someone else's permission, before you start living with courage. By the time you finish these pages, my prayer is that you'll no longer see yourself as ordinary, but as someone ready to live boldly, walk faithfully, and leave an imprint that can never be erased.

CHAPTER 1

THE MARVEL OF MAVERICKS

"Virtually every advancement made by our species since civilization first peeked out of its nest of stone has been initiated by lone individuals, mavericks who more often than not were ignored, mocked, or viciously persecuted by society and its institutions."

- TOM ROBBINS

On a remarkable day in 1924, Gutzon Borglum, the legendary artist and sculptor, gazed from a distance at Mount Rushmore (which was just a mere mountain then) and declared: "American history shall march along that skyline."

Not many took him seriously, for obvious reasons. First, what Borglum saw wasn't what others were seeing. To most people, the mountain was just another mountain in the Black Hills of South Dakota, USA, with its rugged, imposing, and immovable landscape. But to Borglum,

1

it was a blank canvas upon which the story of America could be carved forever.

Borglum envisioned gigantic images of four American presidents (each not less than sixty feet tall), being carved into the mountain to permanently proclaim America's beginnings, progress and greatness. His vision was not only unusual but audacious. No artist in history had ever attempted to carve portraits of such size and symbolic weight directly into a mountainside. Therefore, to most people, the idea bordered on madness.

More importantly, Borglum himself had always carried the reputation of being an eccentric person. He was considered too temperamental, uncompromising, and impossible to pin down. His colleagues and patrons often found him arrogant, especially because of his obsession with monumental art. He never wanted to create "small" works of art; he wanted projects that would "outlast the ages."

He once said: "A monument's dimensions should be determined by the importance to civilisation of the events commemorated." Such thinking made him seem reckless to more conventional artists.

FULFILLING THE VISION

Against all odds, Borglum and his team began the project in 1927, after years of struggling to sell his vision and receive support. To convince backers that he could sculpt giant-sized images into unforgiving granite was almost impossible. He had to wrestle with politics, funding shortages, and fierce opposition. Even when work began, many continued to laugh off the idea. They said it was impossible, a waste of money, the vanity of a madman.

Borglum himself complicated the challenge with his seemingly difficult nature. He quarrelled with funders and was accused of authoritarian methods. But through storms, funding shortages, and endless opposition, he pressed on. Over the next 14 years, more than 400 men laboured under his direction. Pushing the limits of technology at the time, Borglum used controlled explosions of dynamite to remove massive chunks of granite, then refined the details with drills and chisels. Dust and stones rained down as the colossal features began to emerge, from George Washington's resolute gaze, to Thomas Jefferson's profile, to Theodore Roosevelt's glasses, and Abraham Lincoln's solemn eyes. On and on, Borglum's obsession with perfection drove his team relentlessly.

At last, even though the vision outlasted Borglum himself (he died in March 1941, while the project was completed in October), it was eventually accomplished.

Lo and behold, one of history's monumental masterpieces was born. What had begun as the wild ambition of a seemingly stubborn maverick became one of the most fascinating and commanding symbols of national identity ever conceived.

Today, over two million people from across the world make the pilgrimage to this iconic site every year. They come from all walks of life, drawn by curiosity, reverence, and the sheer wonder of standing before something so enormous; something that tells the story of the audacity of a mind that refused to be confined. It is currently one of the most visited and lucrative landmarks in the United States.

THE MESSAGE

I provided the above narrative to prove to you that nobody ever accomplishes anything meaningful and enduring in life without developing the mentality and tenacity of a maverick. It is to let you know that powerful transformations, innovations, and revolutions are never birthed by those who are too conservative or cautious. They're driven by those who dare to see what others call impossible; men and women willing to embrace ridicule, fight against resistance, and cling to a dream no one else can see.

The dictionary defines a maverick as "a person who thinks and acts in an independent way, often behaving differently from what is expected or usual." That definition captures something of the essence, but in truth, a maverick is more than a nonconformist. A maverick is an independent thinker, a rule re-maker, and a relentless doer. Mavericks don't simply challenge the status quo; they disregard it when it stands in the way of progress, truth, or destiny.

Diane Grant once put it this way: *"It is better to walk alone than with a crowd going in the wrong direction."* That sentence captures the heartbeat of every true maverick. They are the men and women who, when faced with the pressure to fit in, decide instead to stand out - even if it costs them popularity, comfort, or approval. Their lives are marked by boldness, by a refusal to be boxed in by tradition, and by a fierce inner conviction that their calling requires a different path.

You've probably seen such people. Perhaps it's the individual who dresses as they please, even when the world sneers that it is unfashionable. Or the colleague who voices an unpopular truth in a meeting, undeterred by disapproval. Mavericks don't wait for permission to be themselves. They carry themselves with an almost electrifying sense of difference. This is not about weirdness for its own sake, but a steady confidence that they were born to walk their own path.

Sadly, this spirit seems rare in our generation. I see many young people who spend their entire time and energy trying to look like who they are not, scrolling endlessly through social media for ways to replicate trends and forgetting their original design. Mavericks reject this imitation game. They dare to say: *"I am not a copy. I am an original."*

MAVERICKS SEE WHAT OTHERS MISS

Consider Elon Musk, the globally acclaimed entrepreneur and inventor. When he started promoting the idea of electric cars, many thought he was delusional. They said electric cars would never compete. People laughed and critics scoffed. Yet, he kept imagining a future where the cars could outpace petrol vehicles and change the climate conversation.

Today, Tesla (which he co-founded) has reshaped the automobile industry, forcing other manufacturers across the world to rethink what they once called "impractical." This happened because Musk didn't just see cars; he saw an energy revolution. That's the marvel of Mavericks. They look at the same facts as everyone else, but their imagination refuses to stop where others stop.

Think of Mark Zuckerberg too, and the revolutionary Facebook. Even as a college student, he envisioned a world where people could connect across borders instantly. Whatever we may think of his creation today, the fact remains that he ignored the voices that said it was impossible or unnecessary. At the time, critics dismissed it as another student distraction, a fad that would fade. Instead, Facebook transformed the fabric of global communication. Mavericks don't merely improve the present; they insist on building futures others are blind to.

History offers countless other examples. When the Wright brothers (Orville and Wilbur) spoke of flying by aircraft, most scientists of their day dismissed the idea as nonsense. Newspapers ridiculed them as chasing mere fantasies. Even the U.S. military initially ignored them. Yet, on December 17, 1903, the two former bicycle mechanics proved everyone wrong. Amid strong winds, their plane lifted off as high as 120 feet, and the world changed forever.

The message here is that mavericks are not defined by their profession but by their perspective. They are like eagles. While other birds peck the ground for crumbs, the eagle soars above, scanning horizons unseen by the rest. Mavericks can walk the same streets, sit in the same classrooms, face the same problems as everyone else, and yet, they notice what others overlook. That's why they make people uncomfortable. They speak of futures others can't yet imagine, and the average mind prefers the comfort of the known.

As Helen Keller once said, "The only thing worse than being blind is having sight but no vision." Mavericks live with vision. They refuse to be chained by "what is." They insist on pursuing "what could be." They are God's instruments to remind the world that possibility is larger than the present, that innovation is born out of holy dissatisfaction.

SEE DIFFERENTLY, STAND DIFFERENTLY

We will shortly be having a detailed exploration of the biblical view of the maverick spirit. However, let me quickly emphasise that Jesus Himself embodied this attribute. Where others saw fishermen, He saw apostles. Where others saw a corrupt tax collector, He saw a gospel writer. Where others saw a broken woman at a well, He saw a revivalist to her city. This is how true mavericks function. They carry God's perspective; they see the seed of greatness where the crowd sees nothing but dirt.

This is why mavericks often walk alone. Their sight isolates them. While others are busy celebrating the present, they are already preparing for the future. But in the end, it is their vision that moves humanity forward. Without mavericks, we would still believe the earth is flat, that slavery is acceptable, that women cannot vote, and that the world's diseases cannot be cured.

Mavericks are seers of possibility. They remind us that every great leap forward in life - from missionary exploits to scientific breakthroughs to artistic masterpieces - began with someone who dared to see what others missed. Renowned paleontologist, David M. Raup, once affirmed this, saying: "Perhaps the only thing that saves science from invalid conventional wisdom that becomes effectively permanent is the presence of mavericks in every generation - people who keep challenging convention and thinking up new ideas for the sheer hell of it or from an innate contrariness".

Essentially, being a maverick means stepping out of the crowd to embrace self-awareness. It means appreciating your uniqueness, trusting your vision, and having the courage to pursue it, no matter how many raised eyebrows or whispered criticisms come your way. Steve Jobs rightly said: "The people who are crazy enough to think they can change the world are the ones who do." History has proven him right. Mavericks are not ordinary people. They refuse to be. To be ordinary is to be swallowed by mediocrity; to be a maverick is to rebel against that smallness and step into greatness.

ALL-ROUND MISSION FIELD

Mavericks are not only found in pulpits or palaces; they shape boardrooms, classrooms, and workshops. They are innovators in technology, disruptors in business, reformers in education. Mavericks prove that the highest form of economic value is not profit but principle; it is vision pursued with integrity, creativity, and courage.

The best mavericks in the marketplace embody integrity, empathy, authenticity, resilience, generosity, and humility. They think long-term, looking to impact lives beyond their balance sheets. They lead compassionately, motivate others with encouragement, and lift those around them. Their leadership is not domination but inspiration. They rebel against the soullessness of business-as-usual and replace it with something human, dignified, and just.

Moreover, what separates a maverick from the rest is not only what they do but how they see the world. Where others see obstacles, they see opportunities. Where others accept conventional wisdom, they question it. Where others chase quick profit, they pursue lasting impact.

They are willing to take bold risks, knowing that every great achievement requires stepping outside the comfort zone. They lead by example, showing through their actions that change is possible. They inspire movements because they are not afraid to stand alone first.

THE CAUSE MAKES THE DIFFERENCE

In 1 Samuel 17, David asked a critical question that provides a powerful insight into the driving force of mavericks. That question was prompted by the hurtful accusation by Eliab, his oldest brother, over his sudden arrival at the battlefield at the time Goliath was intimidating the Israelite army. *"Now Eliab, his oldest brother, heard when he spoke to the men; and Eliab's anger was aroused against David, and he said, "Why did you come down here? And with whom have you left those few sheep in the wilderness? I know your pride and the insolence of your heart, for you have come down to see the battle"* (1 Samuel 17:28). In response, David solemnly said: *"What have I done now? Is there not a cause?"* (1 Samuel 17:29, NKJV).

This reveals the soul of every true maverick. They are not driven by arrogance or rebellion for rebellion's sake. They are not the wayward and disrespectful troublemakers who fight authority out of stubbornness. Rather, they are rebels with a cause. They act because there is something within or around them that demands action. In other words, their rebellion is intentional. It is guided, purposeful, and anchored in destiny. Like David, they are not attention-seekers but people who know that choosing silence and inaction could prove not only devastating but also disappointing and highly regrettable. Their defiance is therefore not the reckless but the righteous kind.

11

To rebel with a cause means choosing the harder path because it aligns with who you truly are. It means burning with fire in your bones for something that matters. Jesus Himself demonstrated this. The Bible says that when his disciples saw the radical way he dealt with those desecrating God's temple, they immediately remembered that it was a fulfillment of the prophecy made about Him. *"Then His disciples remembered that it was written, 'Zeal for Your house has eaten Me up."* (John 2:17). It occurred to them that Christ was not rebelling to make a name for Himself. His rebellion carried holy fire.

That's the kind of rebellion the world needs. In the world today, many are taught to play it safe. We are told to "just manage," "don't talk too much," or "stay out of trouble." Yet nothing great has ever come from blending in. Mavericks are those rare men and women who dare to say, "There has to be more than this."

THE CALL TO DIVINE DISTINCTION

The Apostle Paul urged the believers in Rome, just as God urges every one of us today: *"And be not conformed to this world: but be ye transformed by the renewing of your mind, that ye may prove what is that good, and acceptable, and perfect, will of God"* (Romans 12:2). That is the maverick's anthem. The world has its patterns; it has its compromises, shortcuts,

ADEBAYO NATHANIEL ADEMOLA

and traditions. To follow them blindly is to waste your life. To be transformed, however, is to live with divine distinction.

So, what is your cause? What is it that breaks your heart? Is it the sight of children wasting their lives on drugs? The crushing weight of poverty or abuse? The rampant cases of immorality, indecency, and criminality? Or is it the lack of education or the spiritual emptiness of a generation? I assure you that the burden you feel is not an accident; it is divine. Mavericks do not choose their cause; their cause chooses them. And when it does, they cannot rest until they rise to meet it.

Moses could have stayed in Pharaoh's palace, living in luxury. But when he saw the suffering of his people, something rose in him. His rebellion was initially problematic, uncertain, and full of fear, but God met him in the wilderness and turned his cause into a calling. The same is true for you. You may not have all the answers now, but if the fire is in your heart, don't ignore it.

Once again, remember that to be a maverick is to be an outlier, but not for ego, attention, or rebellion's sake. It is to live with purpose, vision, and holy fire. It is to be willing to carry the burden of being misunderstood because you know your destiny demands it. It is to rebel against smallness, mediocrity, fear, and conformity, and to rise into the greatness God has placed within you.

So, when you hear the word *maverick*, don't think of mere stubbornness. Think of world-changers. Think of men and women who refused to die with their potential buried inside them. Think of those who dared to live differently, and in doing so, gave us a new world to live in.

CHAPTER 2

THE BLUEPRINTS OF BRAVERY

"A maverick may go his own way, but he doesn't think that's the only way."

– ORSON WELLES

We saw in the last chapter that the dictionary defines a maverick as a person who acts independently or thinks differently from the expected or usual way. But, in reality, a dictionary definition can never totally capture the spirit of the maverick: the fire in their bones, the unusual light in their eyes, or their stubborn courage that refuses to bow to mediocrity. Sometimes, they look strange; at other times, they sound unreasonable. In fact, to the average mind, their dreams are ridiculous.

What makes mavericks even more amazing is that they don't all come in the same form. Some are dreamers. Some are fighters. Some are inventors. Some are healers. Some are builders. But what unites them is that they cannot simply accept the world as it is; they must push for what it could be.

Let's examine the distinct dimensions where mavericks challenge convention, so you can discover the space where your own uniqueness thrives.

THE VISIONARY MAVERICK

The visionary is the dreamer who sees what doesn't yet exist. Like Gutzon Borglum, whom we discussed earlier, while others see empty land, they see a city. While others see impossibility, they see a pathway.

Visionary mavericks are simply not content to live within the limits of the present. They have what psychologists call *anticipatory imagination*, which is the ability to vividly picture a different future and then orient their lives toward it, long before anyone else sees what they see. They may be mocked as daydreamers, but their "daydreams" become the blueprints for progress.

Walt Disney, the legendary pioneer of American animation, is another good example here. While he is often remembered for bringing fairy tales to life on screen, his boldest dream went far beyond cinema. When he first proposed the idea of Disneyland, the bankers and investors he approached scoffed at it. To them, the notion of adults willingly paying money to stroll around a park filled with cartoon characters seemed childish, even crazy. One banker reportedly asked, "Who would pay to watch mice and ducks come to life?"

Yet Disney clung tenaciously to his vision. He continued to imagine a place where families could laugh, play, and forget the troubles of the outside world, immersed in an atmosphere of wonder. He kept pouring his heart, creativity, and savings into what others dismissed as a folly.

When Disneyland finally opened in 1955, it was not just a commercial success but the beginning of an empire that continues to enchant millions across the globe. What had been branded a fantasy turned into a cultural landmark that has continued to shape childhood memories and family traditions across generations.

Steve Jobs, co-founder of Apple, was another dreamer who refused to bow to the limits imposed by conventional wisdom. In the 1970s and 80s, computers were bulky machines designed for laboratories, hobbyists, and specialists. Most people could not imagine them sitting on a kitchen table or in a school classroom. Jobs, however, believed that technology should be "beautiful, simple, and intuitive." He envisioned designs that engineers at the time dismissed as impossible. He proposed sleek shapes, uncluttered interfaces, and devices that felt less like machines and more like companions.

His perfectionism and sheer stubbornness not only frustrated colleagues, but also drove innovation. Out of that relentless pursuit came products such as the iPhone, a device that revolutionized not just computing but the very way billions of people live, work, and communicate. Jobs did not merely create gadgets; he reshaped culture, redefined industries, and made technology accessible to the everyday person.

In Nigeria, there was the example of Chief Obafemi Awolowo, who looked at the children of then Western Nigeria and imagined classrooms filled with them, learning freely. It was a radical thought. Free primary education, many argued, was impossible in a country struggling with scarce resources. But Awolowo persisted, insisting that a nation that neglected its children's minds could not hope for progress. Against all odds, he made it happen. Generations later, his legacy lives on. He was called impractical by rivals, but time proved him right.

Visionaries are naturally prone to being ridiculed. Their colleagues may sneer when they begin to speak. Their friends may sometimes whisper that they have lost their senses. Family members may worry that they are wasting their time. But true visionaries are not bothered about the laughter of today because they are busy with the progress of tomorrow. They seem out of place in their own age, not because they are misfits, but because they are already living in a world that has not yet arrived.

18

In summary, visionary mavericks are future-focused, often speaking of realities others cannot yet grasp. Their conversations sound strange because they are describing things that belong to the next chapter of history. They are imaginative, mapping out what is invisible to the naked eye. Where others see emptiness, they trace outlines of possibility. They are often ridiculed because fresh visions nearly always sound "impossible" until they are proven. The laughter of critics is the background music of every groundbreaking idea.

Without visionaries, we would never experience any significant progress. We would drive the same cars, read the same books, use the same tools, and repeat the same mistakes. Every innovation we now take for granted, like the lightbulb, the airplane, and the internet, began as someone's "crazy" dream.

So, if you, dear reader, feel the passion to nurture ideas that others dismiss as foolish, pay attention. That impulse is not madness. It is not arrogance. It is the spark of your maverick DNA, urging you to step forward. It is the beckoning of the future, reminding you that tomorrow belongs to those brave enough to imagine it today.

THE REBEL MAVERICK

Not all mavericks are dreamers who envision a revolutionary future. Some are fighters who cannot bear the weight of injustice. They are disgusted at oppression; their conscience burns when they see wrong. To them, silence feels like consent, and inaction feels like betrayal. These are not rebels for the sake of noise or notoriety, but rebels who rise against broken systems to promote justice and equity.

There are many examples of such in history. You may have heard of Martin Luther, a German monk in the 16th century, who took hammer and nails in hand and pinned his 95 Theses to the church door in Wittenberg. It was a scandalous act of defiance against the colossal Church hierarchy of his day. To speak against the Church then was to risk your very life; yet Luther dared to disturb centuries of unquestioned authority. His protest cracked open the door to what became the Protestant Reformation, a movement that reformed not just the Church but the political and cultural destiny of entire nations.

Centuries later, in Montgomery, Alabama, an unassuming seamstress named Rosa Parks boarded a bus after a long day of work. When asked to surrender her seat to a white passenger, she quietly refused. That single act sent shockwaves through America. It sparked the Montgomery Bus Boycott and fanned the flames of the civil rights movement. Parks did not carry a weapon or lead an army, yet her calm defiance proved more powerful than force. She showed the world that sometimes rebellion begins not with a shout, but with the courage to say "no."

In colonial Nigeria, at a time when most citizens were expected to keep their heads down before British authority, Sir Herbert Macaulay refused to be cowed. Trained as a civil engineer, he could have lived a quiet, comfortable life, but the injustice of the colonial administrators made him restless. He exposed corruption among the leaders and stirred ordinary Nigerians to believe that self-rule was a possibility. The British dismissed him as a troublemaker, especially through his political party and the newspaper that he co-owned, the *Lagos Daily News*. Yet history remembers him as the father of Nigerian nationalism, the man who ignited the first spark of the country's independence.

Rebel mavericks live with deep and often painful tension. In their own time, they are branded troublemakers, agitators, even traitors. Yet history has a way of vindicating them. The same voices once hated are later celebrated as heroes and heroines.

In a nutshell, rebel mavericks are skeptical of authority when it degenerates into oppression. They ask the hard questions others dare not voice. They stir controversy because truth, when spoken aloud, has a way of offending oppressors. They are fuelled by a conviction stronger than fear. Their courage is not the absence of trembling, but the decision to act despite it.

Rebel mavericks speak when silence is safer. They act when passivity is expected. Their fire unsettles the comfortable, but it is precisely this disturbance that births justice. Without them, the chains of oppression would remain unbroken, and history would only be filled with the voices of the powerful. With them, we are reminded that justice often begins with a single act of holy defiance.

THE CREATIVE MAVERICK

These are mavericks who reshape the world not by drawing blueprints for future technologies or fighting injustice, but by daring to reimagine beauty, craft, and creativity itself. They do it through their brushes, pens, fabrics, and rhythms. They are the ones who dare to ask, *what if beauty itself could be reimagined?* This way, they end up shaking the world with wonder – redefining how people see, feel, and express themselves.

Think of Michelangelo. When he lay on his back for four years painting the Sistine Chapel ceiling, he was not just producing art; he was redefining it. The Church wanted simple frescoes. Michelangelo gave them a vision of creation, judgment, and redemption that remains one of the greatest masterpieces in human history. His colleagues called him eccentric, impatient, and even impossible to work with. Yet his refusal to settle for mediocrity gave the world a masterpiece that has outlived popes, kings, and empires.

Leonardo da Vinci was the same. His mind lived on the frontier between art and science, between imagination and impossibility. His notebooks were filled with inventions no one else could fathom. He had sketches of flying machines, submarines, and tanks that were centuries ahead of their time. He simply was not content to paint what others painted, or to imagine what others imagined. Interestingly, most of his visions that were dismissed as "mad" at the time are now recognized as the restless genius of a mind unwilling to be confined by the limits of his age.

Yet, his brilliance was not only in futuristic inventions. With the world-famous *Mona Lisa*, he turned something as simple as a portrait into an eternal mystery. The sitter's half-smile, her gaze that seems to follow you across the room, and the delicate sfumato technique that blurred edges into lifelike softness - all of these redefined what painting could achieve. It was no longer just about recording appearances; it became about capturing soul, emotion, and timeless allure. For over five hundred years, the *Mona Lisa* has drawn millions into her silent enigma, proving that true creativity bends reality itself.

Our country too has witnessed its own pioneers who dared to challenge the limits of creativity. Consider Chinua Achebe, whose *Things Fall Apart* redefined how the world saw Africa. At a time when Western literature reduced Africans to stereotypes, Achebe wrote with dignity, depth, and authenticity. He reshaped not only Nigerian literature but also world literature, forcing readers everywhere to see Africa through African eyes. Following him, writers like Ben Okri carried the torch, blending realism and mysticism in works like *The Famished Road*, which won the Booker Prize and showed that African storytelling could bend the boundaries of form itself.

In visual art, Ben Enwonwu was a trailblazer. His sculptures and paintings fused Western techniques with African identity, asserting Nigerian art on the global stage. His famous portrait of Princess Diana was a mark of international acclaim, but his deeper achievement was showing that Nigerian artistry could speak with universal power. Today, artists like Nike Davies-Okundaye continue that legacy, turning indigenous textiles and motifs into world-renowned works of beauty, teaching generations that tradition and innovation are not enemies but partners.

Even outside fine art and design, Creative mavericks abound. Think of fashion disruptors like Coco Chanel, who threw away corsets and gave women freer clothing. Or designers like our own Deola Sagoe and Lisa Folawiyo, who have taken traditional fabrics, such as *aso-oke* and *ankara*, and turned them into high fashion worn on international runways. These mavericks insist that beauty itself is a form of rebellion, a refusal to live in a dull, unimaginative world.

Essentially, creative mavericks see differently, reimagining what is possible in their field. They often appear eccentric because their minds dwell in unusual spaces.

They redefine norms, shifting what entire industries consider "standard."

If you have ever been told you are "too different," "too quirky," or "too strange," you may, in fact, carry the gift of a creative maverick. That difference may be the seed of your greatest impact.

THE HUMANITARIAN MAVERICK

The Humanitarian maverick is driven by empathy. Where many accept suffering as "just the way life is," these mavericks see an urgent call to bring relief. Their rebellion is not waged with inventions or fiery speeches alone, but with compassion radical enough to shake the indifference of society.

Take Mother Teresa for example, she walked into the slums of Calcutta and began lifting dying men and women from the gutters. To the world, her gestures seemed too small; what difference could it make to bathe one leper, or cradle one orphan? But she saw the face of God in every broken body. That vision transformed what looked like "insignificant acts" into a worldwide movement of mercy. By the time she died, her example had inspired millions to choose love over indifference.

Consider Nelson Mandela too. After twenty-seven years in prison, most people expected him to emerge bitter and ready to exact revenge on those who had contributed to his imprisonment. Instead, he came out speaking of forgiveness and reconciliation. His moral courage did not simply end apartheid; it prevented South Africa from descending into civil war.

You may have also heard of Malala Yousafzai, the Pakistani education advocate, who was shot by extremists for daring to attend school. Instead of giving up, the dogged humanitarian turned her suffering into advocacy for girls' education worldwide. Her courage, driven by compassion for other young girls, forced governments and institutions to rethink the rights of women and children. She ended up becoming the youngest Nobel Prize laureate in history, receiving the Peace Prize at age 17.

Humanitarian mavericks are often misunderstood. Critics sometimes call them naïve and weak. Yet time and again, their stubborn kindness has proved stronger than cruelty. They measure success not in profits but in people healed, fed, educated, and restored.

In essence, humanitarian mavericks are deeply empathetic, carrying others' burdens as their own. They take personal risks for the collective good. They measure success not by wealth but by lives lifted. Humanitarian mavericks prove that compassion is one of the boldest ways to rebel against a selfish world.

THE INNOVATOR MAVERICK

The innovator maverick is driven by a restless desire to improve things, to refine them, and to make them work better than they did yesterday. Where most people accept systems and processes as they are, innovators keep asking, *"What if this could be better?"*

Innovator mavericks are rarely satisfied. They look at a bicycle and see a flying machine. They look at a failing system and see a better way. They endure endless trial and error, yet each failure is treated not as a defeat but as a step towards success.

Thomas Edison is a good example here. In a world ruled by sunrise and sunset, Edison refused to let darkness set the limits of human activity. While others were content with gas lamps and candles, he pictured streets glowing at night, homes and factories powered by steady light.

His journey was not easy. Many told him his ideas were unrealistic, that light could never be made cheap or reliable. Still, Edison kept going, running thousands of experiments until, at last, a filament glowed with promise. His famous words - *"I have not failed. I've just found 10,000 ways that won't work"* - show the spirit that carried him through.

Edison's true genius was not only in inventing the bulb but in building the whole system around it (power plants, wiring, sockets) so electricity could reach everyone. He didn't just give the world inventions; he gave it new possibilities. Like Da Vinci sketching far ahead of his time, Edison proves that progress belongs not to doubters but to dreamers who refuse to quit.

In the 1990s, Jeff Bezos envisioned a bookstore without shelves and a shop without walls; in short, an online marketplace. At first, it seemed ridiculous. Who would order books from a computer screen, trusting them to arrive in the post? But Bezos was not deterred. He built, tested, and refined, and from that seed grew Amazon, a company that not only redefined how we shop but reshaped global commerce. Today, the idea of clicking to buy feels obvious, but only because an innovator maverick refused to settle for the old way.

Innovation, however, is not limited to technologies or markets. Sometimes it is about reimagining the systems of life itself. Wangari Maathai, the Kenyan environmentalist, looked at the barren hillsides of her homeland and saw more than deforestation; she saw opportunity. With determination, she launched the Green Belt Movement, teaching rural women to plant trees and care for the soil. Her vision restored landscapes, empowered women, and sparked a movement that earned her the Nobel Peace Prize.

In Nigeria, we have the likes of Innoson Chukwuma, who looked at the dominance of foreign cars on our roads and asked why Nigeria could not build its own. From that question grew Innoson Vehicle Manufacturing, Africa's first indigenous car company. His factory in Nnewi now produces vehicles tailored to local needs, proving that innovation can thrive even where others see only limitations.

In all, innovative mavericks constantly question systems, probing for better solutions. They are experimental, unafraid of failure, because failure is simply part of discovery. They are practical dreamers, turning ideas into tangible structures, systems, or movements. Innovation is rebellion against stagnation. It is the refusal to accept that "good enough" is truly enough. The innovator maverick reminds us that the world is never finished. It is always waiting for someone bold enough, restless enough, to make it better.

MAVERICKS VS. THE AVERAGE MINDSET

Despite the diversity of their focus, what unites all mavericks is the unique way they see the world. Perspective is everything. Two people can face the same situation, and while one sees a wall, the other sees a door. One sees danger, the other sees opportunity. One hears ridicule, the other hears a challenge. Mavericks consistently interpret reality through the lens of possibility rather than limitation. This is what differentiates the mindset of mavericks from that of the average person.

Let's explore this uniqueness in detail.

RISK AVERSION VS. RISK-TAKING

The average mind clings desperately to safety, like a sailor who never leaves the harbour because the sea is unpredictable. Safety feels comfortable, but it is deceptive. Ships were not built to remain docked, and neither were human beings. Mavericks understand that risk is the birthplace of change. They see that every breakthrough, whether in science, religion, business, or art, requires someone to take a step into the unknown.

CONFORMITY VS. INDIVIDUALISM

The average person blends in, molding themselves to the expectations of family, culture, and society. They become mimics of other people's voices, never discovering their own. Mavericks, however, are willing to stand out, even if it means standing alone.

FIXED MINDSET VS. GROWTH MINDSET

The average person fears failure, avoiding challenges that could expose their weaknesses. They live in the shadow of "what if I fall?" Mavericks, on the other hand, embrace failure as tuition for mastery. They know that every stumble sharpens their skill, deepens their resilience, and clarifies their vision. They understand that failure is not an enemy; it is a teacher.

CONVENTIONAL SUCCESS VS. FULFILLMENT

The average person seeks wealth, status, and the applause of others. They measure success by possessions and positions. But Mavericks know that true success is not accumulation, but contribution. They are driven by meaning, not medals; by purpose, not popularity. Jesus warned in Luke 12:15: *"A man's life consisteth not in the abundance of the things which he possesseth."*

Mavericks align their work with a deeper "why." They ask not just, *"How can I get ahead?"* but *"How can I leave the world better than I found it?"* This is why mavericks transform the world while others merely survive it. They are not superhuman; they simply refuse to settle for the common mindset. Where the average mind sees limits, the maverick sees horizons. Where others follow, mavericks blaze trails. And in doing so, they fulfill not just their potential but their divine destiny.

DISCOVERING YOUR MAVERICK DNA

Now that we've seen the different blueprints of the bravery of mavericks, as well as the unique traits that unite them, let me emphasise that you don't have to be loud to be a maverick. You don't have to be famous, radical, or even fully understood. But I can assure you that, somewhere inside you, there's a spark. A flicker of defiance. A whisper that says, *"This can't be all there is."* That's your Maverick DNA.

Not everyone embodies every type of maverick. Some lead revolutions. Others reshape industries. Some paint the world in new colours. Others heal it with compassion. You might be the visionary who sees what others can't. Or the rebel who refuses to play by broken rules. Maybe you're the creative who turns chaos into beauty. The humanitarian who fights for the forgotten. Or the innovator who builds what's never been built. You might be one. You might be many. You might be something entirely new.

But here's the truth: your maverick identity isn't found by copying someone else's path. It's uncovered by listening to your own unrest. The question isn't, *"Who should I be?"* It's, *"Where do I refuse to settle?"* What makes you restless? What makes you question the norm, challenge the system, or dream beyond the blueprint?

That's where your maverick begins. It might show up in your art, your parenting, your activism, your entrepreneurship, your teaching, your writing, or your leadership. It doesn't need a stage; it needs a stand. And when you find that place where you can no longer pretend everything's fine, where your soul yearns for change, where your voice trembles but speaks anyway, that's where your maverick lives.

You don't have to be all things. You just have to be *your* thing. And the world will be better for it.

CHAPTER 3

THE STANDPOINT OF SCRIPTURE

"Being a Christian executive in Hollywood has proven not to be difficult, but instead, it has contributed to me fulfilling my destiny. Hollywood respects the maverick, the person who's unique and has the confidence to defy the system and everyone who tells them they're wrong in order to follow their vision."

– DEVON FRANKLIN

When Daniel and his friends (Hananiah, Mishael, and Azariah) were brought to Babylon as captives, they were young, far from home, and surrounded by a culture that wanted to reconfigure their identity. New names were given to them, a new language was drummed into their ears, and now new delicacies were placed before them from the king's own table. In a nutshell, they had been handpicked to be re-educated in the ways of Babylon, to eat from the king's table, and to forget the God of their fathers.

35

The delicacies looked rich, tempting, and irresistible. Everyone else ate without question, but Daniel and his friends sensed a major danger - those meals were tied to idol worship and compromise. To partake would mean to silently bow to Babylon's gods, and the Hebrew youths would not. Daniel therefore approached the chief official with humility and asked to be fed with just vegetables and water.

The request seemed not only ridiculous but also very risky. Who says no to luxury when you're a captive? They were offered the best food in the empire; meals prepared for the king himself. Turning that down looked ungrateful, even foolish. Besides, in a culture that prized strength and status, asking for vegetables and water sounded like a recipe for weakness. It defied common sense and nutritional norms of the time. But the Hebrew children knew that was the only way they could avoid being totally immersed in the ungodly Babylonian system.

Still, there was the risky part, which made the chief official hesitate. What if they looked weak and pale compared to the others? To resolve this, Daniel made an interesting offer: "Test us for ten days. Then compare us with the others."

Indeed, ten days later, the result was undeniable. While others grew sluggish from indulgence, Daniel and his friends looked stronger, brighter, healthier. They stood out without trying to. But the difference went beyond appearance. God honoured their maverick choice. He filled them with wisdom and knowledge far above their peers. When they stood before King Nebuchadnezzar, they were found ten times better than all the magicians and advisers in his kingdom. What began with faith at the dinner table ended with influence in the palace.

The decision to reject the king's delicacies wasn't about food. It was about identity. And in choosing to be different, Daniel and his friends became indispensable. They were promoted to higher levels of influence and greatness.

THE DIVINE MANDATE

So, why exactly is the above narrative important to us? Or even better, why are we having the exposition in this chapter? The answer is simple. For too long, many Christians have lived under the false belief that following Christ means blending in, keeping quiet, avoiding conflicts, or rejecting bold, unconventional paths. Some imagine that holiness makes one passive, timid, or overly compliant with the status quo. But nothing could be further from the truth. As the Hebrew children's example shows, from Genesis to Revelation, the story of Scripture is the story of men and women who dared to be different; spiritual mavericks whose lives reshaped nations, overturned idols, and pioneered fresh paths of obedience.

At its heart, Christianity is a maverick faith. To confess Jesus as Lord is to defy the idols of the age. To walk in holiness is to reject the world's crooked patterns. To preach the gospel is to proclaim a new order of life that unsettles the comfortable and liberates the captive. Moreover, the Bible is not a manual for blending in but a mandate to stand out. Throughout Scripture, God calls His people to live differently. He calls us to carry a spirit that challenges darkness, resists conformity, and dares to embody kingdom values in a fallen world.

In essence, from the standpoint of Scripture, believers are not only permitted to be mavericks; we are mandated to be. From the Old Testament, God's call to His people was a call to distinction. Israel's story, in particular, is the story of a nation chosen not to blend in, but to stand apart; a people set aside to reflect God's holiness in the midst of cultures that bowed to idols and chased after vanity.

In Leviticus 18:3, God warned them plainly: *"After the doings of the land of Egypt, wherein ye dwelt, shall ye not do: and after the doings of the land of Canaan, whither I bring you, shall ye not do: neither shall ye walk in their ordinances."* Egypt was the land of their past, Canaan the land of their future, but in both cases, God's command was clear: "Do not copy them." This was not a suggestion but a mandate: their survival and destiny depended on walking a different path.

Again, in Leviticus 20:23, God reminded them that the very reason He was driving out the nations before them was because of their abominable practices. If Israel copied them, they too would be judged. In Deuteronomy 12:30–31, He went further: *"Take heed… that thou enquire not after their gods, saying, How did these nations serve their gods? even so will I do likewise."* God's people were not to experiment with or borrow from the world's systems of worship. To be His was to be distinct.

This call did not end with the Old Testament. In the New Testament, the mandate is renewed and sharpened. Jesus told His followers in Matthew 5:14-16, *"Ye are the light of the world. A city that is set on an hill cannot be hid."* Light is disruptive to darkness. Cities on hills are conspicuous. Salt changes the taste of whatever it touches. The metaphors of discipleship are metaphors of distinction. The Christian life is not camouflage but contrast.

Also, in Matthew 7:13 14, Christ reminds us: *"Enter ye in at the strait gate… because strait is the gate, and narrow is the way, which leadeth unto life, and few there be that find it."* To walk the narrow way is to go where few dare to tread. Mavericks are, by design, minority travellers. Again, Jesus prayed this over His disciples: *"They are not of the world, even as I am not of the world"* (John 17:16). Notice that this is not just a command but a description of reality. If we belong to Christ, we already *are* not of this world. Our calling is simply to live out what we truly are.

39

As we saw earlier, Paul too issued a strong command to the Romans: *"Be not conformed to this world: but be ye transformed by the renewing of your mind"* (Romans 12:2). The word "conformed" pictures being pressed into the world's mould. To resist conformity is to choose the maverick life, living by the Spirit, not by cultural trends. Similarly, Paul reminded the Corinthians: *"Come out from among them, and be ye separate, saith the Lord, and touch not the unclean thing; and I will receive you"* (2 Corinthians 6:17). Separation is not about pride but about intimacy with God. To walk closely with Him requires breaking step with the world. James puts it even more bluntly: *"Friendship with the world is enmity with God"* (James 4:4). In other words, there is no neutral ground – choosing godliness means shunning worldliness, and vice versa!

Peter, writing to scattered believers, used the language of identity: *"But ye are a chosen generation, a royal priesthood, a holy nation, a peculiar people"* (1 Peter 2:9). This is not merely about avoiding sin; it is about bearing God's light. To live set apart is to show forth His praises, to reveal His marvellous light in a darkened world.

Therefore, the scriptural mandate is clear. We are commanded not to conform, but to transform, to witness boldly, to take up the cross, to walk the narrow path, and to shine as light. Mavericks are not anomalies in Christianity; they are the very picture of obedience.

MAVERICKS OF SCRIPTURE

The Bible is a record of God using mavericks to shape history. Time and again, God bypassed the expected and chose the unlikely. He has always delighted in raising men and women who didn't fit the mould.

Let's meet some of them:

NOAH

When the earth was filled with corruption and violence (Genesis 6:11), Noah stood alone as a righteous man in his generation. He dared to believe God's warning of a coming flood, though rain had never yet fallen from the sky. While others mocked his efforts, he faithfully constructed the ark, an act of holy defiance against the unbelief of his age. Noah's obedience was radical. The New Testament calls him a "preacher of righteousness" (2 Peter 2:5), which means his life and labour proclaimed a message of judgment and salvation. His maverick stance preserved humanity and all living creatures. Noah shows us that true faith often requires standing alone, building what others call foolish, and trusting God's word above human ridicule.

JOSEPH

Joseph was a dreamer, and dreamers, as we have seen, are often despised. His brothers hated him for his vision that seemed too profound to them. Betrayed, sold, and imprisoned, he resisted bitterness and compromise. In Potiphar's house, he fought seduction that many would have embraced, to their ruin. In prison, he interpreted dreams with humility and cheerfulness, when he should have been angry and depressed; in Pharaoh's palace, he ruled with wisdom. In the New Testament, Stephen recounts his story as a testimony of God's sovereign plan (Acts 7:9-10). Joseph embodies the maverick who sees destiny in dreams, integrity in temptation, and opportunity in suffering. He teaches us that destiny champions often walk a lonely road, but their determination works wonders.

JOSHUA AND CALEB

When Moses sent twelve spies into Canaan, all saw the same landscape: fertile fields, fortified cities, and giants who towered over them. But their reports could not have been more different. Ten spies returned with trembling voices, declaring, *"We are but grasshoppers in their sight"* (Numbers 13:33). They spread fear among the people, convincing them that the Promised Land was unattainable.

Yet Joshua and Caleb stood apart. They had seen the same giants, but their eyes were fixed on the promise of God, not the size of their enemies. While the others spoke of impossibility, Joshua and Caleb tore their clothes and cried out, *"Let us go up at once, and possess it; for we are well able to overcome it"* (Numbers 13:30). It was a maverick moment; choosing courage when surrounded by cowardice, choosing faith when drowned in fear.

For their defiance, they were nearly stoned by the people. But heaven took note. God declared that all the faithless generation would perish in the wilderness, yet Joshua and Caleb would live to inherit the land. Mavericks often stand alone, but in the end, they stand victorious.

Years later, Joshua proved again that he was no ordinary leader. In the heat of battle against the Amorites, as the sun began to sink, Joshua dared to pray the unthinkable: *"Sun, stand thou still upon Gibeon; and thou, Moon, in the valley of Ajalon"* (Joshua 10:12). And creation obeyed. The sun delayed its setting, the moon halted its course, and Israel won a decisive victory. No day before or since has seen the cosmos bend to a man's prayer in such a way. Joshua's audacity marked him as a maverick who refused to let time itself hinder God's promise.

Caleb's faith, no less, burned with undimmed fire. At eighty years old, when most people would have shrunk back, he stepped forward. The land of giants, the very strongholds that once terrified Israel, was still unconquered. Yet Caleb declared, *"Give me this mountain"*

(Joshua 14:12). He did not ask for easy valleys or fertile plains; he demanded the hardest territory, the place where giants dwelt. And with God's help, he drove them out, proving that faith does not retire, and that true mavericks never lose their edge. Together, Joshua and Caleb remind us that mavericks are not those who ignore giants but those who see them through the lens of God's promise.

DEBORAH

In a time when "every man did that which was right in his own eyes" (Judges 21:25) and no man was found worthy, Deborah was chosen by God as the first female judge and leader of Israel. She sat under the palm tree, dispensing wisdom and divine counsel with uncommon boldness. So charismatic was she that Barak, Israel's military leader, said he wouldn't go to battle without her (Judges 4:9). She shattered the mould of what leadership looked like in a patriarchal culture. She demonstrated that when God calls, gender, culture, and circumstance cannot silence a true maverick.

DAVID

David redefined what a warrior should be. A shepherd boy with a sling, he dared to face a giant armed with sword and spear. Where seasoned soldiers trembled, David declared, *"The battle is the Lord's"* (1 Samuel 17:47). His life was marked by maverick faith: dancing before the ark in undignified joy (2 Samuel 6:14), refusing to kill Saul though he had the opportunity, and writing psalms that still give voice to human longing and divine worship. The Bible calls him a man after God's own heart (Acts 13:22). Yes, he had his moments of stumbling, but he refused to be defeated by constantly seeking God's mercy.

RAHAB

Rahab was a harlot, a woman branded by shame and considered a lowlife; yet she dared to demonstrate remarkable courage and faith in the God of Israel, which ultimately transformed her destiny. Seeing with the eyes of faith what others in her accursed city couldn't see, she hid the spies from Israel on her rooftop. She defied the king's orders and confessed to the spies, *"The LORD your God, he is God in heaven above, and in earth beneath"* (Joshua 2:11). Her scarlet cord became the sign of salvation, foreshadowing the blood of Christ. Though her past was tainted, her faith wrote her name into the genealogy of Jesus (Matthew 1:5) and the "Hall of Faith" in Hebrews 11:31. In essence, Rahab's maverick spirit lay in the fact that she refused to let her past define her future.

RUTH

When Naomi urged her to return to her people and idols, Ruth refused. Unlike Orpah, she clung to Naomi with the powerful words: "Thy people shall be my people, and thy God my God" (Ruth 1:16). With that, she expressed not just loyalty but covenant faith. She broke away from Moabite gods, customs, and prospects of remarriage, stepping into the unknown. As a widow, foreigner, and gleaner, she took the humble path of gathering leftovers, yet her integrity and diligence caught Boaz's eye. Her maverick choice led her into the lineage of David and Christ Himself (Matthew 1:5).

JOHN

John was a very unusual prophet. He wore camel's hair, ate locusts and wild honey, and thundered repentance to the religious hypocrites of his day. While priests performed rituals in the temple, John baptized crowds in the open air, preparing the way for Christ. He rebuked kings for sin, even at the cost of his life. He was such a radical wonder to his generation that Jesus Himself declared, *"Among those born of women there hath not risen a greater than John the Baptist"* (Matthew 11:11). John shows us that true mavericks are heralds of truth who refuse to dilute God's message for comfort or approval.

THE EARLY CHURCH

The early church was born in defiance of both religious tradition and imperial authority. At Pentecost, ordinary men and women were filled with the Holy Ghost, speaking in tongues and declaring the mighty works of God (Acts 2:1–4). To their Jewish contemporaries, this looked scandalous. To Rome, it looked suspicious. But the church was unmoved. They preached Christ crucified and risen, knowing it could cost them their lives.

Their way of life was itself a rebellion against the norms of society. They shared their possessions so no one lacked (Acts 4:32-35). In a world that prized wealth and class, they created a community where slaves and masters broke bread as equals, where women prophesied, and where Gentiles were welcomed into covenant fellowship. The Roman Empire, built on power and hierarchy, could not comprehend such a fellowship of radical love.

When commanded not to preach in Jesus' name, Peter and John boldly replied, *"We ought to obey God rather than men"* (Acts 5:29). These believers endured prison, beatings, and martyrdom, but people testified that they turned the world upside down (Acts 17:6). Hallelujah!

JESUS CHRIST

Jesus Christ is the Maverick of all mavericks. He walked this earth as the greatest disruptor of all. He healed on the Sabbath, touched lepers, spoke with Samaritans, and forgave adulterers. He overturned money changers' tables, exposed religious hypocrisy, and preached good news to the poor. His Sermon on the Mount turned human values upside down. He said blessed are the meek, the persecuted, the merciful (Matthew 5). The New Testament says He came to "destroy the works of the devil" (1 John 3:8), and He did so by laying down His life. The cross was the ultimate maverick act: power in weakness, victory in death, glory in shame. Unlike any other, He defied sin, silenced death, and rose triumphant. He remains the pattern for every holy rebel who dares to follow God against the currents of the world.

GOD STILL RAISES MAVERICKS

This is the ultimate good news for you and me. 1 Corinthians 1:27 reminds us: *"God hath chosen the foolish things of the world to confound the wise."* Therefore, a maverick in God's Kingdom is:

- **Daniel**, who prayed when it was forbidden and was lifted from the lions' den unharmed.

- **The three Hebrew children,** who stood tall when others bowed low, and walked out of the fire without the smell of smoke.

- **Joshua,** who commanded the sun and moon to halt in the sky until victory was complete.

- **Caleb,** who at eighty still demanded mountains, proving that faith never grows old.

- **You**, when you dare to obey God's unusual assignment on your life, even when it defies the expectations of those around you.

However, I want you to note, from the examples above, that God is not interested in misguided noise. He is interested in those who will carry fire with discipline, vision with humility, and conviction with consistency. Romans 12:11 captures the essence: "Not slothful in business; fervent in spirit; serving the Lord."

In just a few words, Paul identifies three pillars of the biblical maverick. These are not traits for mere personal success; they are spiritual anchors for anyone called to walk an unusual path in God's plan, as demonstrated by our various biblical models.

1. Not Slothful in Business: The Call to Diligence

The first mark of a biblical maverick is diligence. God never entrusts transformative assignments to the idle. Mavericks are not those who merely dream; they act. They build, they move, they respond to divine nudges quickly and decisively.

Consider Nehemiah. He was not a prophet, a king, or a priest; just a cupbearer in the Persian court. Yet when he heard about the broken walls of Jerusalem, he was stirred into action. He wept, prayed, fasted, and then sought the king's permission to rebuild. Nehemiah's diligence transformed him from a palace servant into a national leader.

Ecclesiastes 9:10 exhorts us: *"Whatsoever thy hand findeth to do, do it with thy might."* Mavericks live by this principle. They don't wait for ideal circumstances; they step out in faith. They may lack resources, but they never lack resolve.

To be a maverick is to resist the paralysis of procrastination. If God has given you a vision, sitting on it dishonours Him. Movement, however small, is the evidence of faith.

2. Fervent in Spirit: The Fuel of Inner Fire

Diligence without passion quickly becomes drudgery. That's why the second mark of a maverick is fervency. This isn't just human enthusiasm; it is a spiritual flame that burns within, sustained by intimacy with God.

Jeremiah tried to silence his prophetic voice, but he confessed:

"His word was in my heart as a burning fire shut up in my bones, and I was weary with forbearing, and I could not stay." (Jeremiah 20:9)

That is fervency. It keeps you awake at night, restless until you obey. It may make you look strange, even obsessive, to those around you. But fervency is the fuel that carries mavericks through storms, rejections, and delays.

Paul embodied this fervour. Beaten, shipwrecked, imprisoned, slandered — nothing could extinguish his fire to spread the gospel. Mavericks are often misunderstood precisely because their passion makes them unstoppable.

But fervency must be anchored. Fire without control is destruction. Fire surrendered to God is a transformation. The maverick's inner fire must always be tied to heaven's purposes, not personal ego.

3. Serving the Lord: The Anchor of Obedience

The third and most important trait is service. Mavericks are not called to build their own empires. Their boldness is wasted if it is not anchored in obedience to the Lord.

Paul reminds us in Colossians 3:23: *"And whatsoever ye do, do it heartily, as to the Lord, and not unto men."*

Serving the Lord keeps the maverick from becoming self-absorbed. It reminds them that their fire is not for entertainment but for kingdom advancement. The early church, as we already established, was filled with mavericks; ordinary men and women who broke cultural and religious barriers. They carried the gospel beyond borders, not because they sought applause, but because they served God.

A true biblical maverick is defined not by charisma but by conviction; not by rebellion but by responsibility. They may stand out, but they bow down, always aligning their boldness with the will of God.

CHAPTER 4

THE ESSENCE OF ECCENTRICITY

"Taking risks, breaking the rules, and being a maverick have always been important, but today they are more crucial than ever."

- GARY HAMEL

From all we have explored so far, especially the various exploits of mavericks in Scripture and contemporary history, I believe that a holy restlessness must have started stirring in your heart. This chapter is meant to push you further – to make you realise that becoming a maverick is not one option among many; it is the only way to step fully into your God-ordained destiny. Let me begin with the story of "Tesla", the name behind the present global electric car revolution.

When Nikola Tesla began to sketch blueprints in the air with his hands, people called him eccentric and delusional. When he spoke of wireless power and energy drawn from the very earth, they called him mad. Yet it was in that oddness, that refusal to be reasonable, that the future began to take shape.

Tesla was born in 1856 in what is now Croatia. From childhood, he had unusual gifts. He claimed to see flashes of light and entire machines in his mind before building them. This strange ability made people dismiss him as odd, but it was precisely this gift that enabled him to revolutionise electricity.

As at the late 19th century, the world was buzzing with excitement about Thomas Edison's system of direct current (DC). Edison was already a giant, a household name. Tesla, however, insisted that DC was limited and inefficient for transmitting power over long distances. He championed alternating current (AC), which could travel vast distances with little loss. At the time, scientists, investors, and even journalists dismissed AC as dangerous and impractical. Even Edison claimed Tesla's ideas were dangerous.

But Tesla refused to back down. Against all odds, he found support from entrepreneur George Westinghouse, and together they built the first large-scale AC power systems. The turning point came in 1893, when the World's Fair in Chicago was lit entirely by Tesla's AC system. Millions of visitors saw the night sky blaze with electric light, and suddenly the world understood Tesla had been right all along. Not long after, his system powered Niagara Falls, the first great hydroelectric plant in history. The victory was so decisive that today, the entire modern world runs on AC.

What makes Tesla such a compelling maverick is not only his brilliance but his refusal to conform. He was socially awkward, intensely private, and had quirks that made him an outsider. But these eccentricities did not hinder his genius. They seemed almost the mark of it. Of course, history has vindicated him. Today, his name is carried by Tesla Motors, a company that embodies his rebellious spirit of defying the impossible. His alternating current still powers the globe, and his visions of wireless communication have become our everyday reality.

WHAT GREATNESS ARE YOU HIDING?

Maybe you too have had ideas that made your heart leap, but you locked them away because you didn't want people to call you "too much." You swallowed your convictions because you feared, *What will people say?* You shrank back from opportunities because you didn't want to be the only one standing out.

Yet, from the different stories we have shared, it is obvious that mavericks are often accused before they are applauded. Joseph was mocked by his brothers when he shared his dream (Genesis 37). Noah was ridiculed when he built an ark on dry land. David was underestimated when he ran toward Goliath. So, the pattern is always the same - people will call you weird before they call you wonderful.

Ask yourself: *What is the greatness I am hiding?* Is it a book unwritten? A business unbirthed? A ministry unlaunched? A song unsung? The maverick in you is often trapped beneath the fear of others' opinions. But what if the very thing you are hiding is the thing that could save your family, your community, or even your generation?

History tells us that Galileo Galilei was silenced by the Church for claiming the Earth revolved around the sun. They branded him a heretic. Today, he is remembered as the father of modern science. Greatness often appears like eccentricity.

If this is you, then there's a maverick inside you that is waiting to rise.

THE WORLD NEEDS MAVERICKS

The world doesn't just need people; it needs mavericks. Ordinary existence fills the earth, but it is the extraordinary that transforms it. The world needs men and women who carry both boldness and love, conviction and creativity, fire and focus. People who aren't obsessed with fitting in but are consumed with fulfilling their calling.

This generation is noisy, distracted, and confused. Everywhere, voices are clamouring, but not all voices carry weight. We scroll through endless feeds, laugh at recycled jokes, mimic fleeting dances, and yet silently search for meaning. What is missing are authentic voices, souls ablaze with conviction, willing to live differently.

Look around your community. Do you see gaps, brokenness, injustices, or needs that no one seems to notice? That pain you feel is not random; it is your divine compass. Nehemiah wept when he heard Jerusalem's walls were broken down. Esther risked her life to save her people. Martin Luther King Jr. dreamed of a world that judged men by their character, not their colour. Mavericks are not born simply to survive; they are sent to solve problems.

The world needs you. Not the edited version of you that tries to blend in, but the raw, authentic version that shines and stands out. Jesus said, *"You are the light of the world. A city set on a hill cannot be hidden"* (Matthew 5:14). Light is never meant to blend in with darkness; it is meant to expose and transform it.

THE PRESSURE TO CONFORM

Sadly, we live in a world obsessed with conformity. The pressure comes from every angle – from schools, workplaces, churches, families, and especially social media. Instead of creating, many are copying. Instead of thinking, many are parroting. There's a global competition to look like someone else, to speak like someone else, to perform like someone else.

But the truth is that pretending drains the soul. Walking on eggshells for the approval of others strips you of your uniqueness, your voice, and your destiny. You were not created to be a clone; you were designed to be a masterpiece.

Here is Romans 12:2 again: *"Do not conform to the pattern of this world, but be transformed by the renewing of your mind."* To conform is easy. To transform is costly. Mavericks choose transformation over conformity, even when it means being misunderstood.

Shadrach, Meshach, and Abednego refused to bow to Nebuchadnezzar's golden image when everyone else fell prostrate. Their eccentricity landed them in a fiery furnace, but it also attracted the presence of the Son of God. That is the paradox of mavericks: the fire that others fear often becomes their platform for glory.

Look at the climate of our world right now - voices are louder than values; opinions are abundant, but conviction is scarce; talent is buried under fear because safety is rewarded more than originality; and people long for significance but avoid the unknown.

This is why mavericks matter. Without them, the world stagnates. With them, breakthroughs happen. Without them, inventions die in notebooks. With them, industries are reborn. Without them, faith becomes ritual. With them, revival sweeps nations.

Remember what we discovered in Wilbur and Orville Wright's story. When they left bicycle repair for flying machines, newspapers ridiculed them. Engineers dismissed them. Yet, when they took flight at Kitty Hawk, human history changed forever. Today, air travel connects billions of lives daily because two mavericks refused to be reasonable.

ONLY MAVERICKS SPARK CHANGE

Think of the mavericks who've shaped history. Moses, who stood before Pharaoh demanding freedom. Elijah, who confronted 450 prophets of Baal. William Wilberforce, who defied Parliament to fight the slave trade. Rosa Parks who refused to give up her seat.

They all shared one trait, and that is the refusal to conform. Mavericks are willing to be different. They ask uncomfortable questions. They shine light in dark corners. They carve paths through uncharted territories.

At first, mavericks are misunderstood. Then they are resisted. But in the end, they are remembered. Jesus Himself was considered eccentric. His own family once thought He was "beside himself" (Mark 3:21). Yet His refusal to bow to the expectations of Pharisees and politicians became the salvation of the world.

Every breakthrough we enjoy today was birthed by someone who dared to be different yesterday.

YOU DON'T HAVE TO BE PERFECT

Yes, you don't have to be perfect to be a maverick. You don't need to have every answer. You don't need to have it all together. What you need is a willing heart, a readiness to be misunderstood, a courage to be set apart, and a devotion to obey God even when it doesn't make sense.

Peter was impulsive, Moses was insecure, Gideon was doubtful, and Paul was once a persecutor. None were flawless, but all became mavericks. Mavericks rise not because they are flawless but because they are faithful to the fire inside them.

God does not call the qualified; He qualifies the called. The very imperfections you think disqualify you may be the exact vessels through which God's power will shine.

The Bible says, *"The earnest expectation of the creation waits for the manifestation of the sons of God"* (Romans 8:19). This world is desperate, desperate for mavericks who will rise with boldness and be light in the darkness.

And maybe, just maybe, the world is waiting for you. Because someone, somewhere, needs the maverick in you to show up. A student needs your invention. A neighbour needs your courage. A nation needs your voice.

Will you keep hiding your eccentricity, or will you embrace it as the very essence of your calling?

Let's quickly see what happens when anyone chooses to be "normal" or indifferent.

CHAPTER 5

THE NEMESIS OF NORMALCY

"It is impossible to be a maverick or a true original if you're too well-behaved and don't want to break the rules. You have to think outside the box. That's what I believe. After all, what is the point of being on this earth if all you want to do is be liked by everyone and avoid trouble?"

- ARNOLD SCHWARZENEGGER

One of the most tragic stories in history that highlights the downside of "playing safe" or choosing to blend in rather than standing out as a maverick is the story of the prophet recorded in 1 Kings 13. He was young and freshly anointed for an assignment no one else in Israel dared to touch. God had sent him with a message to a corrupt king standing at an altar polluted by idolatry. The instructions were clear, yet strange: deliver the word, refuse to eat or drink in that place, and return by another road. To others, the rules would have seemed eccentric, even unreasonable. But that is how God often works; He marks His messengers with peculiar instructions that set them apart.

The young prophet initially complied with his calling. He proclaimed God's word with boldness, rebuked the king, and denounced his altar. The king raged, stretched out his hand to arrest him and instantly that hand withered. The same king, trembling, pleaded for prayer, and the prophet interceded. Miraculously, the hand was restored. That day, the young prophet stood taller than the king. He had obeyed, and heaven backed him up. The crowd must have murmured in amazement, *who was this daring young man?* He had been different, unbending, a true maverick carrying the fire of God.

Sadly, on his return journey, his courage failed. An old prophet approached him with a smooth story: "*I too am a prophet…an angel spoke to me by the word of the Lord, saying, Bring him back with you to your house that he may eat and drink*" (1 Kings 13:18). The young prophet, probably feeling lonely and weary from his journey, let down his guard. He chose to play safe, setting aside the eccentric instructions God had given him and following the comfortable path of blending into another person's experience and "revelation". He ate and drank, and thereby stepped out of his unique calling and destiny.

On the way back, a lion met him and struck him down. His body lay lifeless, a warning to every generation that when divine destiny is at stake, compromise is fatal.

And the irony is that he was not destroyed when he confronted a king, but when he conformed to a lie. He was not defeated when he was bold, but when he chose safety.

THREAT TO GREATNESS AND DESTINY

The prophet's defeat reveals the nemesis of normalcy. The greatest threat to your destiny is not the opposition you will face but the temptation to play safe or fit in. Mavericks may be misunderstood, mocked, or even hated, but they are never destroyed by standing apart. The true danger lies in blending in. As Theodore Roosevelt, the 26th President of the United States, once said: "Far better it is to dare mighty things, to win glorious triumphs, even though checkered by failure, than to take rank with those poor spirits who neither enjoy much nor suffer much, because they live in the grey twilight that knows not victory nor defeat."

Consider Joseph. What if he had let go of his dreams the moment his brothers rejected him - when they mocked his vision and tried to silence his voice? What if, in the face of betrayal and isolation, he had chosen to "play it safe"? Worse still, what if he had taken the shortcut of compromise with Potiphar's wife, trading integrity for temporary comfort? His destiny would have been derailed. The palace would never have known his wisdom, and Egypt would never have seen his rise.

Now think of David. What if he had allowed his brother's harsh words to shrink him? What if he had chosen the path of least resistance, doing things the "normal" way - waiting in line, staying quiet, letting fear dictate his actions? We wouldn't be speaking of his bold stand against Goliath, nor the deliverance of Israel that followed. His courage to defy the expected is what made history.

The point here is that while it may seem attractive to play safe, playing it safe will not get you very far; in fact, it may land you on the opposite side of God's plan for your life.

Of course, I understand that we live in a world that glorifies "fitting in." From childhood, we're taught not to be "too much": *don't talk too loud, don't dream too big, don't stand out too far.* Schools, workplaces, and even churches can reward compliance more than creativity, conformity more than conviction. Yet, as we have seen, every breakthrough in history has come from someone willing to step outside the comfort of normal.

Normalcy feels safe, but it is a prison. It lulls you into thinking that peace comes from avoiding attention, when in truth, peace comes from fulfilling purpose. The young prophet's tragedy teaches us that the moment you silence your eccentric edge (the divine difference in you), you step onto dangerous ground.

THE SUBTLE PRISON OF COMFORT ZONE

At first glance, the comfort zone looks harmless. You follow the rules, stay out of trouble, do just enough, and everyone nods approvingly. Nobody criticises you. Nobody expects much from you. Life feels stable. But beneath that surface lies a deadly reality: "safe" is expensive. It costs you your dreams, your joy, your growth, and perhaps even your destiny.

Comfort zones are like old shoes: familiar, reliable, and easy to slip into. But wear them too long, and they pinch, wear out, and slow you down. What once felt comfortable becomes a cage. Consider the dangers:

1. Stagnation

Refusing to step out of comfort is like running on a treadmill; there's plenty of motion, but no progress. You may keep busy, but you're going nowhere. Growth demands change, and change demands discomfort.

2. Inability to Deal with Change

If your life is confined to the predictable, surprises will break you. The moment your routine is disrupted, panic sets in. But those who practice stepping beyond comfort zones become agile. They adapt. They interpret unexpected turns not as disasters but as new paths.

3. The Death of Growth

Life's greatest lessons often arrive in unfamiliar territory. Creativity thrives in disruption. When you refuse new challenges, you plateau. Like an artist who never dares to use a new canvas, your work becomes repetitive, predictable, and lifeless.

Jesus warned about burying our talents (Matthew 25:14–30). The servant who hid his one talent in the ground thought he was being safe. But safety turned out to be disobedience. His caution cost him his destiny.

THE HIDDEN COSTS

Many justify mediocrity with a shrug: *"At least I'm safe. I have nothing to lose."* But that is a tragic lie. Playing safe is not neutral; it is costly. And the real danger is not just what it does to you, but what it denies others.

When you choose to blend in:

- You silence your voice.

- You suppress your gifts.

- You rob the world of solutions entrusted to you.

Someone's breakthrough, encouragement, or healing may be waiting for you to rise. Your courage could ignite another's hope. Your innovation could birth an industry. Your testimony could save a soul. When you retreat, others remain stuck. When you hide, others lose hope.

Think of Moses at the burning bush. When God called him to deliver Israel, his instinct was to shrink. *"I am slow of speech... please send someone else"* (Exodus 4:10–13). Moses mistook smallness for humility, but it was actually destructive fear. God wasn't after eloquence; He was after obedience. When Moses eventually said yes, a nation walked free. Imagine if he had clung to his excuses; Israel's story might have remained a tale of slavery.

That is why the Apostle Paul could declare with unflinching confidence: *"I can do all things through Christ which strengtheneth me"* (Philippians 4:13). It wasn't bravado; it was defiance against smallness. Mavericks live by this truth: the danger is not in attempting too much and failing, but in attempting too little and succeeding. As Marianne Williamson famously wrote, *"Our deepest fear is not that we are inadequate. Our deepest fear is that we are powerful beyond measure."*

Playing small dishonours the One who placed greatness within you.

WHY WE CLING TO NORMALCY

So, why is normalcy so alluring? One reason is because our brains are wired to avoid uncertainty. Psychologists tell us the human mind associates predictability with survival. Darkness unsettles us because the unknown carries risk. Yet, in trying to avoid uncertainty, we risk never truly living.

Think of Israel in the wilderness. God had promised them a land flowing with milk and honey. Yet, because of fear, they circled the desert for forty years. The wilderness represents normalcy: safe enough to survive, too small to thrive.

Mavericks, however, interpret discomfort differently. Where others see threat, they see possibility. They understand that uncertainty is not a void but a canvas. For them, discomfort is not an enemy but a midwife that helps to birth growth, creativity, and transformation.

Another reason many also cling to normalcy is because society often celebrates the wrong voices. The young prophet in our story must have felt that tension: watching the king honour him after the miracle, then hearing another prophet contradict God's word. Whose voice should he trust? The one that seemed popular and convenient.

Our world still works this way. Social media rewards conformity with likes, while silencing those who speak uncomfortable truths. Corporations reward employees who blend in, not those who question the status quo. Political systems often exalt the charismatic follower of trends rather than the bold voice of conviction.

But history tells another story. The ones who shape the future are never the ones who bow to applause. They are the ones who speak the truth even when nobody claps.

BREAKING THE GRIP OF NORMALCY

Ralph Waldo Emerson once said, *"To be yourself in a world that is constantly trying to make you something else is the greatest accomplishment."* These words cut to the core of the battle between normalcy and authenticity. Playing safe feels comforting, predictable, and socially acceptable. It promises peace, but it delivers mediocrity. It nudges us, *"Don't risk. Don't stand out. Don't be odd."* Yet, that very whisper has lulled multitudes into living lives that vanish unnoticed into the grey wallpaper of routine existence.

This is why Dr Myles Munroe once said, "The wealthiest place in the world is not the gold mines of South America or the oil fields of Iraq or Iran. They are not the diamond mines of South Africa or the banks of the world. The wealthiest place on the planet is just down the road. It is the cemetery. There lie buried companies that were never started, inventions that were never made, bestselling books that were never written, and masterpieces that were never painted. In the cemetery is buried the greatest treasure of untapped potential."

Look around. Our world is not short of educated men and women, professionals, influencers, and experts. It is overflowing with sameness. Everyone has something to say, but so few have something original to declare. Everyone is skilled, but few are daring. In such a crowded marketplace of voices and abilities, the only way to stand out is not by cautious improvement but by daring disruption.

To be a maverick is to embrace the audacity of uniqueness. Mavericks are the ones who refuse to blend into the background. They don't merely upgrade existing ideas; they birth entirely new paradigms. They are like the stars in a night sky: while others are part of the dark canvas, they pierce through with light.

Still, we cannot deny that being a maverick is lonely. The young prophet must have felt it, walking away from the king's feast, refusing food, traveling by another road. His path was eccentric, set apart, strange. That's often what obedience feels like.

But loneliness is not the same as abandonment. God never leaves those who dare to stand apart. Elijah, despairing in his cave, thought he was alone; yet God had preserved seven thousand others who had not bowed to Baal. Mavericks may feel alone, but they are part of a hidden army.

As Soren Kierkegaard said, *"The crowd is untruth."* To live by truth often means walking away from the crowd. And sometimes, that's the only way to keep your calling intact.

EMICATE: THE SPARK BEYOND NORMALCY

To rise above normalcy, mavericks practise what we may call *Emicate*, the art of sparking something new by stepping outside what is safe.

1. The Thrill of the Unknown

For mavericks, the unknown is not a dark alley but an unexplored adventure. Like Abraham, who left his homeland not knowing where he was going, they embrace journeys without maps.

2. Comfort Zones as Cages

What others treat as havens, mavericks recognise as prisons. Predictability breeds mediocrity. True transformation always begins outside the boundaries of what is known.

3. Discomfort as a Midwife

Growth hurts. Muscles ache when stretched, minds resist new patterns, and hearts tremble at risk. But every stretch is labour pain for a stronger self.

4. The Courage to Fail and Try Again

Mavericks redefine failure. Recall Thomas Edison's famous quote: *"I have not failed. I've just found 10,000 ways that won't work."* Mavericks know each failure is tuition paid for wisdom.

5. The Spark of Creativity

Routine suffocates imagination. Disruption awakens it. Every leap into the unfamiliar is an invitation to innovation.

6. The Ripple Effect of Inspiration

Mavericks don't just pioneer for themselves; they clear paths for others. Their courage is contagious. By daring to rise, they empower countless others to do the same.

RISE FROM NORMALCY

Now, the clarion call comes to you: arise and take your rightful place in destiny. To remain normal is to forfeit greatness, to dim your light, and to silence your voice.

Jesus declared: *"Ye are the light of the world. A city that is set on a hill cannot be hid"* (Matthew 5:14). Your design is visibility, not invisibility. God is not glorified when you shrink to fit others' comfort zones. He is glorified when you rise, shine, and embody the fullness of who He made you to be.

The nemesis of normalcy is real. But it can be defeated when you dare to obey the inner call, when you choose faith over fear, when you step beyond the familiar into the vastness of possibility.

To be a maverick is not merely to resist the pull of the ordinary but to rebel against it; to shine so brightly that darkness has no choice but to scatter.

Your life is not just your own. It is a torch, a vessel, a city on a hill. Do not let the nemesis of normalcy bury it under the rubble of fear. Rise. Shine. And let the world see what God has placed in you.

CHAPTER 6

THE CAPACITY OF CONQUERORS

"Along with the differences that abide in each of us, there is also in each of us a maverick, the darling stubborn one who won't listen, who insists, who chooses preference or the spirited guess over yardsticks or even history."

– MARY OLIVER

Having walked through the stories of the remarkable mavericks in the preceding chapters, and perhaps recalling others you've admired from history, Scripture, or even your own life, you may find yourself thinking: *"That could never be me."* Maybe you marvel at their courage, their bold choices, their visible impact. You cheer them on, yet quietly convince yourself that greatness is reserved for a select few - the flawless, the fearless, the specially chosen. Deep down, you wonder if you'll ever measure up.

Perhaps you're thinking:

- "I'm not bold enough."

- "I don't have the right support."

- "I've made too many mistakes."

- "I'm too old."

- "I'm too young."

- "It's too late for me."

If those words feel familiar, let me stop you right there. Here's the truth that dismantles every excuse you've ever rehearsed: God has already placed everything you need inside you. Yes, everything. You are not a half-finished sketch waiting for someone else to complete you. You are not an empty vessel hoping to be filled someday. You are already equipped, already wired with divine potential, already carrying within you the seeds of greatness that God Himself planted.

That restless hunger to create, that unshakable urge to speak, that drive to build, to lead, to serve, to change things is not random. It's not wishful thinking. It is divine. It is your inner fire.

Think about it. Fire is chemically present in wood but invisible until ignited. As soon as the spark comes, everything transforms. In the same way, your life may have looked quiet, even ordinary, but the spark of faith and obedience can awaken the blaze God buried in your soul.

And here's the turning point: the moment you stop doubting it, the moment you stop silencing it, the moment you stop waiting for someone else to give you permission, and you begin to step out with courage, that inner fire erupts, and everything changes.

Mavericks don't sit around waiting for validation. They don't ask the world's permission to shine. They ignite what God has already deposited in them. They rise when it would be easier to shrink. They dare when it would be safer to hide. And that's what makes them world-changers.

CRAFTED WITH CAPACITY

We earlier considered an assertion by business thinker, Gary Hamel, where he observed that challenging norms, stepping into uncertainty, and embracing bold individuality have always mattered, but that they are even more so in today's rapidly changing world. While Hamel was speaking of business and innovation, the truth he voiced reflects a much deeper and older revelation. Long before modern strategists coined such insights, Scripture had already made it clear that God designed you with a built-in capacity.

God specifically told Jeremiah: *"Before I formed thee in the belly I knew thee; and before thou camest forth out of the womb I sanctified thee, and I ordained thee a prophet unto the nations"* (Jeremiah 1:5). This truth applies to everyone, including you. And the principle is simple: capacity is not determined by the user, but by the manufacturer. A blender that carries the label *1.5 litres* does not do so because the owner measured and guessed its size. That stamp of capacity comes from the one who designed and produced it. In the same way, your Creator knows exactly what He has built into you - your strength, endurance, resilience, imagination, breaking point, and potential. You may underestimate yourself, but Heaven does not.

Paul writes in Ephesians 3:20, *"Now unto Him that is able to do exceeding abundantly above all that we ask or think, according to the power that worketh in us."* Isn't this interesting? It says God does not work in your life according to what is around you, but according to what He has already placed in you. The extraordinary things God intends to accomplish through your life will not come as an external shipment from somewhere else; they will be released from within you. In other words, you are already equipped. The treasure is already deposited. All you need is to recognise and activate this inbuilt power. Mavericks don't crawl when God has given them wings!

Look again at Genesis 1:26–27. God paused and said, *"Let us make man in our image, after our likeness..."* Unlike the seas or the stars, which He spoke into existence, humanity was fashioned with intention and deliberation. You were not mass-produced. You were handcrafted. And God's design was precise.

God's purpose for specially creating you is twofold:

1. **To Reflect His Nature.** You carry the imprint of His creativity, wisdom, love, and leadership DNA. The impulse to design, to imagine, to problem-solve, and to build are not random quirks of personality. They are traces of divinity. You are wired to think, dream, and innovate like God!

2. **To Reign, Not Just Exist.** Genesis 1:28 reveals God's mandate to humanity, including you – especially if you have surrendered your life to Him: "Be fruitful, and multiply, and replenish the earth, and subdue it: and have dominion…"

Dominion here is not about domination or oppression; it is about stewardship, management, leadership, and innovation under God's authority. Adam's very first assignment was naming the animals; a task that required confidence, imagination, and capacity. God entrusted Adam with responsibility because He had already placed in him the ability to carry it out.

Even when sin fractured creation and marred that design, the story did not end there. Through Christ, the blueprint was restored. Ephesians 2:10 declares, *"For we are His workmanship, created in Christ Jesus unto good works, which God hath before ordained that we should walk in them."* The Greek word for workmanship is poiēma, from which we derive "poem." This means that you are God's poetry in motion, His very masterpiece. Simply put, you are not a mistake to be managed, but a work of art being restored to glory!

This is why excuses like *"I'm not bold enough"* or *"It's too late for me"* collapse in the face of truth. The manufacturer's stamp is still on you. The capacity is still intact. Mavericks know that greatness is not about external circumstances lining up; it is about the inner fire awakening.

God has already written creativity, resilience, courage, and authority into your very design. So, the question is not, *"Do I have what it takes?"* The real question is, *"Will I trust the One who made me enough to use what He placed within me?"*

Think of Moses. When God called him to confront Pharaoh, his first reaction was to protest: *"I am slow of speech and slow of tongue."* (Exodus 4:10). In other words: *"My capacity is too small for this assignment."* But God's reply was firm: *"Who has made man's mouth?"* (Exodus 4:11). In other words: *"Moses, the manufacturer knows exactly what He put inside you. Don't tell me what you lack; trust what I have deposited."*

Or consider Helen Keller, who was deaf and blind from early childhood. She was told by many that her life would be limited to darkness and silence. Yet she became a prolific author, activist, and lecturer, shaping conversations about disability and human dignity for generations. Her story reminds us that capacity is not dictated by human perception but by divine potential.

And then there is you. Every time you silence yourself with, *"I can't,"* you argue with the One who made you. Every time you shrink back because of failure or fear, you reduce your capacity to your own measurements instead of God's.

PROOF OF INNER CAPACITY

So, what is this inbuilt capacity or inner fire that we're talking about? It is that stubborn spark that refuses to die, no matter how much life tries to snuff it out. It is the passion you can't bury, the problem you can't ignore, the dream that keeps you awake at night. It's that restless voice within you, saying, *"There has to be more than this."*

Paul understood this when he wrote to Timothy: *"Fan into flame the gift of God, which is in you"* (2 Timothy 1:6, NIV). Notice that he didn't say, *"Wait for God to give you something new."* He said, "Fan into flame what's already there."

That means you are not empty. You are not ordinary. You are not behind schedule. You are carrying something holy, powerful, and disruptive within you. Mavericks are those who refuse to let that fire smoulder. They stir it, feed it, and let it blaze.

Below are some clues that you have inner capacity:

1. You Have Breath in Your Lungs

This may sound basic, but it means a lot. The very fact that you are alive is proof that your assignment is not over. Job 33:4 says, *"The Spirit of God has made me, and the breath of the Almighty gives me life."* God does not waste His breath. If you are breathing, you are carrying capacity.

2. You're Restless for More

That gnawing sense of "I was made for more than this" is not arrogance; it is calling. It's your capacity knocking on the door of your soul. The Israelites groaned in Egypt not because food was scarce but because destiny was greater. Your restlessness is divine agitation pushing you toward your maverick assignment.

3. 3. You Get Ideas That Won't Let You Rest

Do you have a business idea, a ministry vision, a book, or a solution that you couldn't shake off? Even when the resources are missing, the thought won't die. That persistence is a sign of capacity stirring. Philippians 2:13 reminds us, *"For it is God who works in you to will and to act in order to fulfill His good purpose."*

4. You're Drawn to Help, Solve, or Lead

Do people look to you for advice? Do you see solutions where others see problems? Do you feel an itch to lead, fix, or innovate? That's not a coincidence; it's potential leaking through. Mavericks notice what others ignore and refuse to leave it as it is.

YOU CARRY TALENTS AND NATURAL GIFTS

The things that come naturally to you are not random; they are clues to your God-given capacity. Scripture reminds us in 1 Peter 4:10, *"Each of you should use whatever gift you have received to serve others, as faithful stewards of God's grace in its various forms."*

Some people write with ease, others calculate numbers like second nature, some sing as if Heaven placed a harp in their lungs, and others can organise chaos into order without breaking a sweat. These natural inclinations are not accidents; they are God's fingerprints on your design.

Often, what feels ordinary to you is extraordinary to others. David only thought he was good with a sling until that talent brought down a giant and opened the door to kingship. Joseph's knack for interpreting dreams was not just a quirky trait; it was the gift that preserved nations.

Your talents may look small, but they are keys. They point to the inner capacity God has placed in you for influence, impact, and innovation. Don't dismiss them; develop them. What you steward faithfully today could be the very tool God uses to set you apart tomorrow.

ASK GOD TO SHOW YOU WHAT'S INSIDE

This is the surest way to discover your inner capacity. You cannot know a product better than its manufacturer. The designer always knows the original wiring, hidden features, and intended purpose. In the same way, you cannot fully know yourself without revelation from your Creator.

Note also that you won't find your maverick calling by comparing yourself to others or chasing trends. You find it when you go back to the One who made you. If God wired you to question, lead, or build new paths, then spend time with Him asking why.

Psalm 139:14 (KJV) "I praise thee; for I am fearfully and wonderfully made; marvelous are thy works; and that my soul knoweth right well."

But many don't yet know that "full well." They're still questioning their wiring, their voice, their place. That's okay. But don't stop there. Go back to the blueprint. Ask God: "Why did you make me like this? What am I supposed to do with this fire?" And don't be surprised when the answer comes with both direction and peace.

If you're reading this and you've struggled to see yourself as a maverick, pause. You don't need to be loud, aggressive, or rebellious to qualify. You simply need to recognize that God has called you to walk differently, to think with conviction, and to act with courage in the areas He's entrusted to you.

Being a maverick is not about performing; it's about aligning. God's blueprint for you may not look like anyone else's. But it's not lost. It's not broken. It's waiting. And the sooner you embrace that He designed you on purpose, the sooner you can live from that place with peace, power, and clarity.

Several years ago, a young man's Ford vehicle broke down on the side of a road. Confident in his knowledge of cars, and especially this particular model, he went to work under the bonnet. He tried everything he could think of. Each time, he returned to the driver's seat to turn the key, but the engine refused to start. Sweat poured, frustration mounted, but nothing worked.

Then a large limousine pulled up, and out stepped an elderly man. He quietly observed for a while before pointing out a very specific adjustment the young man needed to make. At first, the young man was skeptical.

He had already tried so many "more obvious" fixes, and this suggestion seemed too small and insignificant to matter. But out of exhaustion, he finally gave it a try. To his surprise, the car roared to life instantly.

Stunned, he asked, "How did you know what to do?"

The old man smiled and replied, "My name is Henry Ford, and I invented this car."

Here's the lesson: only the manufacturer truly knows the product. Likewise, only God fully knows what He has deposited inside of you. Friends may guess. You may even experiment with your skills and passions. But to really unlock your God-given capacity, you need His revelation. He knows the gifts, callings, and capacities He placed in you, some of which may still be hidden beneath layers of doubt, fear, or inexperience. God Himself invites us in Jeremiah 33:3: *"Call unto me, and I will answer thee, and show thee great and mighty things, which thou knowest not."*

When you ask God to reveal what He has already placed inside you, you position yourself to move beyond self-doubt and into destiny. He may highlight strengths you've overlooked, burdens you've ignored, or dreams you've been too afraid to chase. But His guidance always unlocks potential.

You can say this prayer: *"Dear God, open my eyes to the gifts and strengths You've placed in me. Show me what You designed me to carry and accomplish on this earth."*

In Case You Still Feel Ordinary or Inadequate...

Think of Moses. When God called him, his first response was insecurity. "O my Lord, I am not eloquent... but I am slow of speech, and of a slow tongue" (Exodus 4:10). He tried to convince God to pick someone else. Yet this same stammering man stretched out his rod and parted the Red Sea (Exodus 14:21), bringing a whole nation out of slavery.

Think of Gideon. When the angel of the Lord appeared to him, calling him a "mighty man of valour" (Judges 6:12), he was hiding in fear, threshing wheat in secret. He argued that he was the least in his father's house and from the weakest clan (Judges 6:15). Yet God saw capacity in him. Empowered by divine strategy, Gideon defeated an enemy army of thousands with only three hundred men (Judges 7:7).

Think of David. To his family, he was just a shepherd boy, the one left in the fields while his brothers stood before Samuel. Yet the Lord told Samuel, *"Man looketh on the outward appearance, but the Lord looketh on the heart"*

(1 Samuel 16:7). That overlooked boy became the giant-slayer who toppled Goliath (1 Samuel 17:50) and later the king of Israel.

Think of Esther, an orphan girl raised by her cousin. She seemed insignificant in the Persian palace, yet when her people faced annihilation, she chose courage over comfort. *"If I perish, I perish"* (Esther 4:16), she declared. Her boldness saved a nation.

Do you see the pattern? Mavericks are not flawless heroes. They are ordinary men and women who refused to let weakness define them. They stepped out with what they had, trusting God to multiply it. You may feel too ordinary, but ordinary is God's favourite raw material.

Don't measure yourself by what you see today. A seed looks small, but inside it lies a forest. You may not look like the maverick God is calling you to be, but the DNA of a conqueror is already in you. 2 Timothy 1:7 declares, *"For God has not given us a spirit of fear, but of power and of love and of a sound mind."* That is your default setting: power, not fear; capacity, not limitation.

The world teaches you to measure capacity by comfort. God measures it by calling. And your calling is clear: to rise as a maverick, to dare where others fear, to lead where others follow, to shine where others hide.

CHAPTER 7

THE RESPONSE OF REBELS

"Maverick is a word which appeals to me more than misfit. Maverick is active, misfit is passive.
- ALAN RICKMAN

From the outset of this journey, we have established that every generation is marked by its mavericks, men and women who refuse to sit quietly in the safety of conformity. They are not content to observe the routines of normalcy from the sidelines; instead, they rise with a different spirit; the spirit of rebels. And we have also seen that to rebel in this sense is not to live in lawlessness, but to resist the dull weight of mediocrity and inaction.

Now that you've realised that the maverick spirit lives and pulsates right inside of you, the next important step is to activate it because that's the only way you can make an impact. There is a difference between recognising potential and activating it. The maverick spirit within you is useless until you activate it. Untapped potential is like a treasure buried deep in the earth; precious, but doing no good to the world. Therefore, you must rouse that part of you that dares to rise when others shrink back, that chooses bold action when the majority stay silent.

Mere dreams and desires do not change the world; action does. As someone rightly says, *"If you want to make your dreams come true, the first thing you have to do is wake up."* Talking about dreams is easy. Posting inspirational quotes is convenient. Sharing goals with friends feels rewarding. Yet unless a dream translates into daily action, it remains a wistful fantasy.

THE TIME TO START IS NOW

To activate the maverick spirit is to move from words to works, from potential to performance. It is to decide that your life will no longer be governed by the limits of the crowd but by the call of God and the conviction within. Rebels are defined not by their dreams but by how they respond to this divine call. And the call rarely comes when you feel ready; it usually arrives when you are least prepared.

That is why the call to activate the maverick spirit is urgent. To delay is to betray the very potential God has planted within you. Jesus Himself warned His followers not to hide their light under a bushel, but to let it shine before all men. A light concealed is as good as darkness; a vision unexpressed is as powerless as if it never existed. Consider Nehemiah, who wept at the ruins of Jerusalem's walls. Many saw the destruction; only he resolved to act. His journey was fraught with opposition, ridicule, and threats, yet his determination turned vision into reality. Likewise, Noah faced mockery as he constructed a vessel for a flood no one believed in. What distinguished them was not merely the ability to see differently but the courage to act differently.

Of course, this activation sometimes begins in discomfort. Growth does not blossom in ease. It comes when a person allows holy unrest to push them beyond what feels safe. Like an eagle that stirs her young out of the nest, life itself disrupts our comfort so we can spread our wings. To awaken the rebel spirit is to accept this stirring, to step into unfamiliar territory, and to dare to live in obedience to a call that frightens yet liberates.

If there is one great enemy of rebellion with purpose, it is delay. The rebel does not wait for the approval of the crowd or the certainty of conditions; they respond in the urgency of now. Opportunities do not linger forever. Time, like a flowing river, carries them downstream, out of reach of those who hesitate.

The language of procrastination is deceptively soothing: *"I'll do it one day. I'll begin when I'm more prepared. I'll start after I've figured everything out."* Yet that mythical "one day" rarely arrives. Waiting for perfect timing is like chasing the horizon, an endless pursuit that leaves you motionless. If you do not plant the seed today, you will not see the harvest tomorrow. The longer you delay, the dimmer your fire burns until eventually it flickers out.

Rebels understand that action, even imperfect action, is better than endless contemplation. By stepping forward, they invite momentum, and momentum births possibility. Every small decision creates ripples; every step sets off a chain of growth. History remembers not the dreamers who sat idle, but the doers who stepped forward when others hesitated. The time to act is not tomorrow. The time is now.

Procrastination is more than wasted time; it is wasted life. The tragedy of many lies not in what they failed to desire, but in what they failed to begin. People often comfort themselves with the idea that they are "waiting for the right moment." Yet in truth, they are paralysed by fear: fear of failure, fear of rejection, fear of stepping out of line.

Rebels pierce through this paralysis with courage. Think of Caleb and Joshua, who stood against the murmuring crowd that insisted Israel could not take the

Promised Land. While others delayed and doubted, they responded with urgency: *"Let us go up at once and possess it."* Their boldness distinguished them as men of a different spirit. The rest waited for a "better day" that never came; Caleb and Joshua claimed a future because they acted in faith when others froze.

Procrastination is rebellion against destiny, but urgent action is rebellion against fear. And the question stands before every person: will you be among those who excuse themselves with "one day," or among those who answer with "today"?

TURNING YOUR DREAMS INTO REALITY

To do this, first comes clarity. A blurred vision paralyses, but a sharp one propels. Define what you want. Don't say, *"I want success."* Say, *"I will build a business that provides sustainable jobs for fifty people within five years."* Don't say, *"I want to be healthier."* Say, *"I will run three kilometres every morning before work."* Clarity births commitment.

Next comes planning. Dreams without strategy collapse under pressure. Nehemiah rebuilt Jerusalem's walls not by mere prayer but by meticulous preparation. Rebels use frameworks like SMART goals — Specific, Measurable, Achievable, Relevant, Time-bound. This doesn't make them ordinary; it makes them effective.

Then comes breaking the vision into steps. Big dreams can suffocate; small goals empower. If you want to write a book, start with one page a day. If you want to learn a skill, commit to thirty minutes daily. Small steps compound into seismic shifts.

Above all comes consistency. Mavericks don't wait for motivation; they cultivate discipline. Daniel prayed three times daily, not occasionally but habitually. Paul wrote letters in chains. Joseph remained faithful in prison as he had been in Potiphar's house. Rebels move when tired, they persist when mocked, they create under pressure. They build momentum that mediocrity cannot match.

Most importantly, comes alignment. Rebels don't just chase ambition; they pursue assignment. Many plans may fill the human heart, but only the counsel of the Lord will stand (Proverbs 19:21). At the core of a true rebel is not arrogance or self-reliance but identity anchored in God. A rebel who is aligned to God's will is unstoppable. Without Him, ambition becomes vanity, courage becomes recklessness, and rebellion becomes rebellion for its own sake. But with Him, the rebel's fire is directed, purified, and empowered.

Joseph's life exemplifies this. From betrayal to imprisonment, his journey seemed like a detour from destiny. Yet his unshakeable faith in God turned every trial into training. His identity was not in his coat of many colours, his position in Potiphar's house, or even his power in Pharaoh's palace. It was in God who was with him. That identity steadied him through temptation, suffering, and eventual exaltation.

When rebels know who they are in Christ, they can stand boldly, even in obscurity. They can endure delay without despair, because they know the Author of their story. They can defy the crowd without fear, because their validation comes from heaven. Identity in God transforms rebellion from a personal ambition into a divine mission.

In summary, to activate your rebel spirit:

- **Identify your burden.** What injustice, need, or gap keeps you awake? That's your cause. Moses saw an Egyptian beating a Hebrew slave and could not look away.

- **Refuse the herd instinct.** If everyone is chasing quick money, chase meaningful impact. If everyone is silent in corruption, dare to speak. Mavericks do not mirror; they model.

- **Talk to God about your burden.** Rebels often carry weights too heavy to bear alone. Prayer turns burden into blueprint.

- **Start small.** Mavericks are not born on stages— they are formed in obscurity. The three Hebrew boys first said no to the king's food before they said no to his idol. Start where you are.

- **Find fellow rebels (Networking).** Isolation kills fire. As iron sharpens iron, so rebels sharpen rebels. A lone spark flickers; a cluster ignites.

WHY YOU NEED TO NETWORK

Even mavericks need allies. Every maverick needs a tribe. Lone rebellion may spark attention, but only shared conviction sustains a movement. Proverbs 27:17 reminds us, "Iron sharpeneth iron; so a man sharpeneth the countenance of his friend."

Consider Paul. The Church initially doubted him because of his past, but Barnabas believed in him, vouched for him, and helped launch his ministry (Acts 9:27). Mavericks may stand apart, but they are never called to stand alone.

Build a network that sharpens you, not one that dilutes you. Surround yourself with those who provoke courage, not complacency. True mavericks multiply mavericks. History shows us that every revolution, every turning point, was carried forward not by one person alone but by communities of like-minded souls who gathered around a cause. Martin Luther King Jr., the iconic civil rights leader, never marched alone. His power was magnified because thousands chose to walk beside him, their collective footsteps echoing across history. Mavericks are never islands; they are catalysts that draw others into the fire of change.

The starting point is often close to home. Look first to your immediate circle — classmates, colleagues, neighbours, and church members. Within familiar environments lie hidden allies who may share your vision or support your cause in unexpected ways. What you need may already be within reach, waiting for you to recognise and nurture it.

In today's digital world, social media extends this circle far beyond geographical borders. A thoughtful, humble message of admiration can open doors to mentors and collaborators you might never meet otherwise. A simple, respectful note that says, *"I admire your work in [area]. Could you share one piece of advice with me?"* carries more weight than a flood of insincere requests. Mavericks know that boldness in reaching out often reaps unexpected rewards.

But connection cannot be one-sided. To build networks that endure, you must add value. Share resources that could help others, spread encouragement generously, and exchange ideas freely. Rebellion grows stronger when it is nourished by generosity rather than drained by self-interest. Networking that thrives is one where both sides leave richer, not just in opportunity but in spirit.

And never neglect the art of follow-up. A single conversation can fade like a spark unless you tend to it. Something as simple as saying, *"I enjoyed our conversation about [topic]. Here's an article you might find useful,"* shows attentiveness and strengthens the bond. Over time, these small gestures weave the fabric of trust, transforming acquaintances into allies and allies into a tribe.

THE DISCIPLINE OF REBELS

If passion is the spark, discipline is the fuel. Many begin with enthusiasm but fade when challenges arise. Rebels, however, are not swayed by fleeting emotion. They marry passion with discipline, creating resilience that outlasts difficulty.

Discipline means choosing what you want most over what you want now. It is rising early to work on your vision, even when sleep beckons. It is refusing distractions that promise immediate pleasure but sabotage long-term fulfillment. It is keeping commitments when no one is watching, because integrity matters more than applause.

This is not to say the journey is without setbacks. Rebels stumble too. They face moments of weariness, seasons of doubt, and the sting of failure. But unlike others, they rise again. They treat failure not as a verdict but as a teacher. Every mistake becomes a lesson, every obstacle a stepping-stone. This is the disciplined defiance of rebels: they refuse to quit.

THE COURAGE TO BELIEVE

Ultimately, the response of rebels is a response of courage. Courage is not the absence of fear but the decision to act despite it. It is built through small, consistent choices: speaking up when silence is safer, starting even when uncertainty looms, persevering when quitting feels easier.

To say yes before you feel fully equipped is the essence of courage. David did not wait until he was trained in the king's armour before facing Goliath. He went with what he had, a sling, a few stones, and faith in God. To delay would have been to surrender. To act, even with little, was to rebel against fear.

Confidence is not an accident. It grows when you dare repeatedly. The first time may feel clumsy, the second uncertain, the third shaky. But every attempt strengthens your resolve until boldness becomes natural. Like muscles built through resistance, courage develops through repeated acts of defiance against fear.

Rebels know that greatness does not come to those who wait politely for permission; it comes to those who rise with holy defiance and say, *"If God is with me, I will*

101

not sit still." Their courage becomes contagious. Their faith inspires others. Their lives echo through history, not because they were perfect, but because they dared.

Rebels also resist the need for validation. They are not crippled by waiting for applause or permission from others. Jesus Himself endured ridicule, slander, and rejection, yet He pressed forward in obedience to His Father. Mavericks understand that alignment with God's purpose matters more than the approval of the crowd. Their yes is not conditional on public support but anchored in conviction.

ANSWERING THE CALL

The response of rebels is urgent, disciplined, faith-filled action. They awaken the maverick spirit, embrace the now, refuse the paralysis of "one day," and say yes to the call even before they feel ready. They discipline themselves, anchor their identity in God, and grow in courage until fear bows before faith.

Every generation waits for such rebels. And the question remains: will you be one of them? Will you rise today, not tomorrow? Will you rebel against comfort, conformity, and fear, and instead embrace courage, discipline, and purpose? The world does not need another dreamer who waits. It needs a rebel who responds.

CHAPTER 8

THE CONTINUATION OF CONQUEST

"Do not cringe and make yourself small if you are called the black sheep, the maverick, the lone wolf. Those with slow seeing say that a noncomformist is a blight on society. But it has been proven over the centuries, that being different means standing at the edge, that one is practically guaranteed to make an original contribution, a useful and stunning contribution to her culture."

- CLARISSA PINKOLA ESTES

It is one thing to activate your maverick spirit, but quite another to sustain the tempo and keep the fire burning. Indeed, the most difficult part of the maverick journey is not beginning but continuing. Many start with fire but falter when storms arise. To keep the maverick spirit alive requires intentional cultivation of inner strength. Faith is the anchor, reminding you that obedience to God's call is never in vain. Courage is the armour, shielding your heart against fear and intimidation. Consistency is the fuel, transforming your small, faithful actions into monumental impact.

BECOME AN UNUSUAL SOLUTION PROVIDER

Being an unusual solution provider helps in sustaining your maverick spirit. It means offering answers or strategies to problems in ways that are unexpected or different from the norm. It's about breaking away from conventional thinking and finding creative, sometimes unconventional methods that others might overlook.

This doesn't mean just being different for the sake of it, but it's about applying unique perspectives to problem-solving. It might involve using tools, techniques, or strategies that are less common but more fitting for the specific challenge at hand. It's about finding smarter ways to address issues, using creativity, resourcefulness, and innovation.

Being an unusual solution provider can be especially valuable in environments where problems are complex or where conventional methods have failed. It involves thinking outside the box, being open to experimentation, and having the courage to try new things, even if they initially seem risky.

Mavericks aren't just thinkers, they are problem-solvers. And not just any kind of problem-solvers, but unusual solution providers. What sets them apart is their ability to look at a problem from an entirely different angle. While others may see obstacles, Mavericks see opportunities.

WALKING YOUR OWN PATH

It can be really scary to walk alone, but what should actually scare you more is the thought of walking someone else's path. It's easy to get caught up in the advice from books, videos, and the countless people you talk to about their career journeys. While all of this can give you new ideas, the truth is, your path is completely unique to you. You can't follow someone else's footsteps and expect to find success and fulfillment the same way they did.

The only person who can decide what truly matters to you, and what connects with you deeply, is you. It's about figuring out what makes you feel alive and passionate, and then creating your own journey from there.

It doesn't matter how successful you are at following someone else's path if, deep down, you don't feel fulfilled. True success comes when your journey aligns with what feels right for you inside.

When you're on the wrong path, you'll sense it. Your body and mind will give you clues. For some people, it feels like a tightness in their chest, a heat that builds up, signaling that something isn't in sync with who they really are.

That's your inner compass trying to steer you in the right direction. Listen to those feelings, they're there to help you find your own unique path.

Why do you need to walk your own path?

- It brings peace

- You're satisfied even with little achievements

- You become an inspiration to others

- You have joy doing what you want

- You'll own true success

CULTIVATING THE MAVERICK'S INNER STRENGTH

A maverick's inner strength is the foundation of their unique character, enabling them to rise above adversity, challenge norms, and pursue greatness with unwavering resolve. This strength is not merely a product of natural talent or inherited traits; it is shaped by life's trials, personal growth, and deep reflection. While some individuals may possess innate qualities such as resilience or emotional intelligence, it is the way these traits are developed and refined through experience that truly defines a maverick.

The journey of cultivating inner strength often begins in adversity. Mavericks are frequently shaped by difficult circumstances, be it financial hardship, personal loss, or social exclusion. These experiences can either break a person or build them into someone who defies the odds. For mavericks, such challenges become the forge in which their determination and resolve are strengthened, allowing them to transform pain into purpose.

A strong sense of purpose is central to a maverick's resilience. This internal compass, discovered and nurtured over time, guides them through setbacks and failures. Unlike a mere desire for success, their purpose is rooted in a deeper mission - whether to create change, inspire others, or fulfil a calling that others might overlook. This clarity gives them the strength to persevere, learn from mistakes, and continue moving forward even when the path is uncertain.

Emotional intelligence and self-control are also vital components of a maverick's inner strength. Their ability to manage emotions - both their own and those of others - allows them to remain calm under pressure and make thoughtful decisions. Rather than being overwhelmed by fear or anger, they channel these emotions into constructive energy. Their discipline enables them to stay focused and act with intention, regardless of the emotional climate.

While inner strength is often seen as a solitary trait, mavericks thrive with the support of meaningful relationships. Encouragement from family, mentors, and like-minded peers reinforces their belief in their mission and provides additional strength during challenging times. Ultimately, a maverick's inner strength is a dynamic blend of environment, experience, and conviction, cultivated through hardship, sustained by purpose, and expressed through resilience and emotional clarity.

MABSOOT: FINDING HAPPINESS IN OTHERS' JOY

Rather than viewing others' achievements as a threat, mavericks see them as a celebration of shared progress. Their belief is rooted in the idea that when others thrive, the world becomes richer, more vibrant, and full of possibilities for everyone.

This mindset is reflected in their generosity. Mavericks with Mabsoot are generous not only with material resources but also with their time, encouragement, and emotional support. They celebrate others' victories as if they were their own, offering loyalty and enthusiasm without envy. Their fulfillment comes from seeing others rise, and they become pillars of support in both personal and professional circles.

Mavericks often take on the role of mentors, driven by a deep sense of purpose. They uplift others not for personal gain, but because it aligns with their belief in collective growth. When someone they've guided reaches a milestone, their joy is heartfelt and sincere. For them, helping others is not a transaction; it's a mission rooted in the conviction that every effort contributes to a greater good.

This trait also influences how mavericks build communities. Their joy in others' success fosters environments of collaboration rather than competition. They create spaces where people feel valued, supported, and inspired to grow. The positivity they radiate becomes infectious, encouraging others to adopt the same spirit of mutual celebration and shared achievement.

Ultimately, Mabsoot represents a profound shift in mindset, from individual triumph to collective victory. mavericks understand that success is not a limited resource, and they embrace the interconnectedness of human progress. Their happiness is amplified, not diminished, by the joy of others. In a world often driven by comparison, mavericks with Mabsoot stand as beacons of generosity, unity, and true fulfillment.

ACCOY: DEALING WITH PAIN AND DISAPPOINTMENT

Pain is a shared human experience, but mavericks respond to it in a unique way. Rather than allowing pain to halt their progress, they use it as fuel to propel themselves forward. This transformative ability is known as *Accoy*, the power to soothe pain through dreams and visions. For mavericks, their aspirations offer hope and meaning, helping them navigate adversity with purpose and resilience.

Instead of merely enduring pain, mavericks channel it into growth. They understand that setbacks and disappointments are not roadblocks but opportunities for personal development. Pain prompts reflection and refinement, sharpening their focus and strengthening their resolve. Their dreams remain constant, but their approach evolves, becoming more intentional and determined with each challenge they face.

Accoy also involves turning pain into purpose. Mavericks do not allow their struggles to define them; they use them to inspire others. Their journey becomes a testament to perseverance, and their pain becomes a source of strength. This mindset enables them to stay committed to their goals, even when others might be overwhelmed by hardship.

Dreams serve as a source of healing for mavericks. In moments of chaos or emotional turmoil, their vision acts as a guiding light, offering clarity and comfort. These dreams are deeply personal and often tied to a greater calling. Visualising their goals helps them shift focus from what hurts to what's possible, creating a sense of peace and control amidst uncertainty.

Ultimately, Accoy is a profound trait that empowers mavericks to transform pain into progress. It allows them to find solace in their dreams, grow through adversity, and inspire those around them. Rather than being defined by hardship, Mavericks rise above it, using their inner vision to heal, evolve, and pursue greatness with unwavering strength.

VICTORAS: PERSEVERING FOR VICTORY

Victoras is the maverick's approach to perseverance, not just enduring hardship, but living victoriously through it. For mavericks, perseverance is more than persistence; it's a mindset that transforms obstacles into stepping stones. They don't merely survive challenges; they use them as fuel to live with purpose, strength, and triumph.

This victorious living is rooted in an unshakeable commitment to keep going, even when the odds are against them. Mavericks understand that success rarely comes easily. Their path is often marked by rejection, failure, and pain, yet they persist with grit and determination. They see setbacks not as defeat but as temporary hurdles, knowing that resilience is what sets them apart.

Central to Victoras is the mindset of a champion. Mavericks don't adopt a victim mentality; they face adversity with confidence and self-belief. They understand that their response to difficulty shapes the outcome. Each failure becomes a lesson, each challenge an opportunity to grow. For them, success is not just about reaching a goal; it's about how they journey through the struggle.

Mavericks embrace struggle as an essential part of growth. They see hardship as a refining process, much like a sword forged in fire. The long nights, the battles, and the setbacks all contribute to their strength and adaptability. Rather than avoiding discomfort, they lean into it, knowing that true victory is born from perseverance through pain.

Living victoriously also means celebrating every win, no matter how small. Mavericks recognise that progress is made in steps, and each one deserves acknowledgement. These moments of triumph reinforce their belief that perseverance pays off. By embracing struggle, maintaining a champion's mindset, and honouring each victory, mavericks embody Victoras, a life of resilience, purpose, and unstoppable forward motion.

REFIRING YOUR
DETERMINATION TO EXCEL

Mavericks refuse to settle for mediocrity; they are driven by an internal fire that compels them to exceed expectations and constantly evolve. Their ambition is established in self-mastery, not external validation, and they thrive on challenges that stretch their capabilities.

Even the most determined mavericks face moments when their fire dims. Whether through burnout, setbacks, or emotional fatigue, they recognise that motivation isn't constant. What sets them apart is their ability to re-ignite that flame. They reconnect with their purpose, reflect on their journey, and seek fresh inspiration to fuel their drive. Re-firing is a conscious act, one that restores energy and renews focus when the path gets tough.

Excellence is a non-negotiable for mavericks. They don't just aim to do things well—they aim to do them exceptionally. Their relentless pursuit of improvement keeps them innovating, refining, and elevating their performance. Mavericks like Steve Jobs and Serena Williams exemplify this mindset, showing that true greatness lies in the details, the discipline, and the refusal to rest on past achievements.

Growth is central to the re-fire process. Mavericks embrace discomfort, knowing that stepping outside their comfort zone is where transformation happens. They actively seek new challenges and opportunities to learn, ensuring their fire never fades. This mindset keeps them energised and forward-focused, as seen in figures like Elon Musk, whose ventures span industries and redefine boundaries.

Resilience is the backbone of refiring. Mavericks don't crumble under pressure; they rise. They use failure as fuel, criticism as clarity, and setbacks as stepping stones. Their ability to bounce back, recalibrate, and keep pushing is what enables them to achieve what others deem impossible. Every obstacle becomes a chance to deepen their resolve and sharpen their focus.

Finally, mavericks inspire others through their example. Their determination, energy, and refusal to settle spark motivation in those around them. By striving for excellence, they create a ripple effect, encouraging others to pursue greatness too.

TEN AREAS TO CULTIVATE TO
SUSTAIN YOUR MAVERICK SPIRIT

To wrap up this chapter, here are ten vital areas you must nurture to keep your maverick fire burning and conquering:

1. Spiritual Growth

The foundation of every lasting rebellion against mediocrity is a life anchored in God. Spiritual growth ensures that your actions are not merely driven by ego or ambition, but by enduring truths that transcend circumstances. Mavericks must carve out rhythms of prayer, meditation, and Scripture, because in these disciplines they receive strength that outlives applause. Without spiritual depth, rebellion can devolve into noise, but when anchored in faith, it becomes purpose-filled and unstoppable.

2. Self-Awareness

Every maverick must understand their unique wiring. To compare yourself constantly with others is to invite exhaustion. David could not fight in Saul's armour because it did not fit him; he won his battles with a sling and a stone. Likewise, you must discern how you are built, your gifts, temperament, and calling and walk faithfully in that lane. Mavericks thrive not by imitation but by authenticity.

3. Mentorship

No one sustains greatness in isolation. The wisdom of mentors shortens your learning curve and spares you unnecessary mistakes. Moses had Jethro, who taught him the art of delegation. Timothy had Paul, who poured into his faith and leadership. Mavericks should never despise guidance. A wise tutor for each season of life is a gift from God, a compass that helps you navigate uncharted paths.

4. Skill Development

Passion without skill soon fizzles out. Mavericks distinguish themselves not just by daring but by doing well. Deliberate practice, intentional learning, and the honing of craft separate amateurs from masters. A violinist who rehearses daily becomes an artist; a writer who disciplines their pen shapes nations. Skill turns raw potential into refined excellence, and excellence commands attention.

5. Character Building

Talent may open doors, but only integrity keeps them open. Mavericks must cultivate character because charisma can impress for a moment, but integrity sustains for a lifetime. In a world dazzled by quick success, those who hold fast to honesty, humility, and faithfulness shine brightest. Your rebellion loses power if it lacks credibility. Guard your character like a treasure, for once it is lost, it is difficult to regain.

6. Education

To sustain a maverick spirit, the mind must remain sharp. Formal and informal education both play their role. Formal study disciplines your thinking, while informal learning through books, conversations, travel, or even failure stretches your imagination. Mavericks are perpetual learners. They never assume they know it all; instead, they approach each season with the humility of a student and the hunger of an explorer.

7. Leadership and Service

Mavericks must resist the temptation of selfish ambition. True leadership is rooted in service. Jesus declared that the greatest among us must be servants, and His own life embodied this truth. Mavericks lift others as they climb, transforming rebellion from a personal pursuit into a communal movement. By serving, they multiply their impact and inspire others to carry the torch.

8. Emotional Maturity

Greatness is often undone not by external enemies but by internal storms. Anger, fear, discouragement, and pride can sabotage a maverick's journey if left unchecked. Emotional maturity is learning to master your spirit, to respond wisely rather than react rashly. Joseph, despite betrayal and false accusation, managed his emotions and rose to govern a nation. Mavericks must develop resilience, learning to stand steady when everything around them shakes.

9. Positive Relationships

The company you keep shapes the spirit you sustain. Mavericks must intentionally nurture relationships with those who inspire and challenge them, while pruning away voices that drain, discourage, or distract. Iron sharpens iron, but rust corrodes. Choose companions who sharpen your convictions, not those who dull them. In the end, your tribe becomes the environment where your spirit either flourishes or fades.

10. Vision and Goal Setting

Finally, a maverick must keep sight of the horizon while walking faithfully through daily steps. Vision provides direction, while goals provide structure. Without vision, life becomes aimless; without goals, vision remains a mirage. Mavericks must regularly refine their vision, setting clear goals and aligning their daily actions with their long-term purpose. In doing so, they ensure that each step carries them closer to the destiny for which they rebelled in the first place.

Together, these ten areas form the scaffolding that sustains a maverick life. Ignore them, and the fire may dim. Cultivate them, and your spirit will not only endure but blaze brighter with each passing season.

FINAL WORDS

YOU WERE BORN TO WALK THIS PATH

I believe you've come this far in reading this book because the Holy Spirit has begun to quicken your spirit to your true calling. Perhaps you've always felt that you were never designed to fit neatly into the small boxes others call "normal life." Maybe you've been waiting for someone to say it's okay to be intense, passionate, and deeply driven. Hear it now: it is more than okay. But this boldness, this inner fire, is never the end goal. It is always a tool. Your vision, voice, and courage are meant to serve a greater assignment, the purposes of God.

From the very beginning, God shaped you with intention. That restlessness you feel, that sense of difference, isn't an accident. It is calling. Yet, the maverick path is not always smooth. You may be misunderstood, even rejected. You may find yourself the only one in the room willing to speak the truth. But you are not alone. God walks with those who walk with Him. What you need is not applause or permission—it is alignment with the One who designed you this way.

And here lies the warning: you can be bold, yet misaligned. You can be visionary, yet driven by ego or pain instead of the Spirit. Mavericks without surrender end up in rebellion, mistaking stubbornness for courage. King Saul began with promise but lost his place because he acted outside of God's instruction (1 Samuel 15). Your strength is not in how far you push ahead, but in how closely you walk with the God who sends you.

That is why surrender matters. The most powerful mavericks are not the loudest, but the ones who know how to kneel. In surrender, pride is broken, vision is purified, and direction is clarified. Too many burn out because they try to work for God without sitting with Him. Your fire will not last if it is disconnected from the Vine. True maverick living is not just about platforms, it is about purity. It is about slowing down enough for God to shape your voice, your message, and your movement.

The world does not need more noisy rebels; it needs mavericks who are aligned. A life of purpose is not one that dazzles the crowd but one that honours the blueprint of the Creator. It is lived faithfully, even in obscurity, because heaven is watching and legacy is being written. This is the decision before you: Will you shrink back to be accepted, or will you rise to carry responsibility? Will you blend in to avoid resistance, or will you stand up to bear light?

Thank you for walking this journey. Thank you for searching your heart, asking hard questions, and daring to face the truth of who you're becoming. That takes courage. You may not have all the answers, but you don't need them to move. Mavericks trust God with the next step and show up anyway. If this book has helped you see even a glimpse of your divine design, then it's done its job.

This is not the end, it's the beginning. Let what you've read become what you live. Revisit these words when you forget who you are. Share them with someone who feels out of place. And when the weight of walking differently feels heavy, don't shrink; stand taller. Your voice matters. Your obedience matters. Stay submitted. Stay listening. Stay on fire. The maverick life won't always be easy. But it will always be worth it.

PRAY THIS PRAYER

Father

Thank you for creating me with intention.

Thank You for the fire You placed in my spirit, the drive to stand, the vision to see what others miss, and the courage to go where others won't.

Forgive me for the times I've doubted that design, hidden it, or tried to shrink myself to fit into spaces you never called me to.

Today, I surrender my life, my gifts, my voice, and my boldness to You.

Shape my steps. Refine my motives. Direct my path.

Use my life, not just to challenge what's broken, but to build what honors You.

Keep me humble, but never timid.

Keep me on fire, but never reckless.

Keep me aligned, so I never run ahead of Your will.

Let me live not for recognition, but for obedience.

Let me serve, lead, and speak from a place of deep connection to Your heart.

In Jesus' Name,

Amen.

www.ingramcontent.com/pod-product-compliance
Lightning Source LLC
Chambersburg PA
CBHW071516120626
46550CB00006B/2244